KU-007-660

Watch out! common
mistakes that
students make in the
exams. Make sure
that you don't fall into
the same traps!

Playing in a competition or team sport can be a **physical** challenge: you will be burning calories, your heart rate will be increasing into the target zone, and you will be improving your levels of fitness, endurance and overall health. Competing is a **mental** challenge, which has the benefits of helping you to forget about other worries in your life and relieving stress. And as part of a team you will be mixing with others, working with others, developing teamwork and cooperation. You will often make friends through playing in a team. These are all **social** benefits.

Aesthetic appreciation can be defined as seeing the beauty in the performance. It can be found in any activity and provides the mental benefit of satisfaction. If you are asked to provide an example of aesthetic appreciation, remember that great unstoppable shot in football that scored a goal, or a diving catch in cricket, or the winning stroke in the Wimbledon final.

Results Plus
Watch out!

Remember how to explain aesthetic appreciation. In some past papers the worst answers have been to this question!

Results Plus
Build Better Answers

Which of the following best describes a mental benefit of exercise?

A Meeting new people
B Losing weight
C Relieving stress
D Improved performance

Question 1 is often this type of question. Even if you don't know the answer, you can work it out by a process of elimination. You can rule out **meeting new people**, **losing weight** and **improved performance** so the answer is: **C relieving stress**.

Test yourself

1 Which of the following statements best describes a physical benefit of exercise?

   A Enjoying playing for your team.
   B Gaining an aesthetic appreciation of movement.
   C Feeling better about body shape.
   D Improving body shape.

2 The benefits of taking part in physical activity are listed below.

   a Write each benefit in the correct column of the table.
   b Add your own example for each. Each example should be related to a particular sport that you know.

   Benefits:

   - contribute to enjoyment of life
   - contribute to good physical health
   - help the individual feel good
   - improve performance
   - increase fitness
   - increase self-esteem and confidence
   - make new friends
   - mix with others
   - meet old/current friends
   - mental challenge
   - physical challenge
   - develop teamwork/cooperation
   - relieve and/or prevent stress and tension
   - work with others
   - aesthetic appreciation

Physical	Social	Mental (or psychological)

Results Plus
Build Better Answers

Possible benefits of taking part in exercise can be grouped as

A Mental
B Physical
C Social
D Contribute to good physical health

Which of the benefits of exercise named above, A, B, C or D, would best match each of the following statements?

1 I participate in exercise to relieve stress.
2 I joined a local sports club so that I could get out more and meet people.
3 I restarted my training after Christmas to try to lose weight.

In this question, the options have to be matched; once again, this can be done by a process of elimination. Do the obvious ones first. 'Contribute to good physical health' is not a heading, it is a physical benefit. So you can discount it. 'Stress' and 'mental' fit together nicely so **A** matches **1**. 'Meet people' and 'social' fit nicely too so **C** matches **2**. Which leaves **3** to fit with **B**.

So the correct answers are: **1 A, 2 C, 3 B**.

Exam Question Reports past exam questions with real data on how well students answered them.
- Red shows the proportion of students who scored low marks (under 35%)
- Orange shows the number of students who did okay
- Green shows the number of students who did well (70% of marks or higher).
They explain how students achieved top marks so that you can do the same.

1.1 Healthy, active lifestyles

1.1.1 Benefits

1.1.2 Influences

1.1.3 Exercise and fitness

1.1.4 Physical activity

1.1.5 Your personal health and wellbeing

1.2 Your healthy, active body

1.2.1 Physical activity

| X | ? | ✓ | Describe the different body types and explain the effect of each on participation and performance | 46 |

| X | ? | ✓ | Outline why and how expected and optimum weight varies according to height, gender, bone structure and muscle girth; explain how this may affect participation and performance in physical activity | 48 |

| X | ? | ✓ | Explain the terms anorexic, obese, overfat, overweight, underweight; explain how they may impact on achieving a sustained involvement in physical activity | 48 |

| X | ? | ✓ | Explain the effects of smoking and alcohol on general health and on physical activity | 51 |

| X | ? | ✓ | Know about different categories of drugs and the effects they may have on health, wellbeing and physical performance and why some performers might risk using them | 51 |

| X | ? | ✓ | Identify risks associated with participation physical activities, and explain how to reduce these risks to better maintain wellbeing | 54 |

1.2.2 Cardiovascular system

| X | ? | ✓ | Understand the immediate and short-term effects of exercise and physical activity on the cardiovascular system | 56 |

| X | ? | ✓ | Understand the long-term effects of regular exercise and physical activity on the cardiovascular system | 56 |

| X | ? | ✓ | Understand the impact of rest on the cardiovascular system | 58 |

| X | ? | ✓ | Understand the impact of diet on the cardiovascular system | 58 |

| X | ? | ✓ | Understand the impact of recreational drugs on the cardiovascular system | 58 |

1.2.3 Respiratory system

| X | ? | ✓ | Understand the immediate and short-term effects on the respiratory system of participation in exercise and physical activity | 59 |

| X | ? | ✓ | Understand the long-term effects of regular exercise and physical activity on the respiratory system | 59 |

| X | ? | ✓ | Understand the impact of recreational drugs on the respiratory system | 59 |

1.2.4 Muscular system

| X | ? | ✓ | Understand the role of the muscular system during physical activity and how the major muscle groups benefit from particular types of physical activity | 62 |

| X | ? | ✓ | Understand the role of muscles in movement | 62 |

| X | ? | ✓ | Understand the immediate and short-term effects on the muscular system of participation in exercise and physical activity | 65 |

| X | ? | ✓ | Understand the long-term effects of regular exercise and physical activity on the muscular system | 65 |

| X | ? | ✓ | Understand the potential for muscle injuries through exercise and physical activity and know common techniques for treatment | 65 |

| X | ? | ✓ | Understand the impact of rest, diet and performance-enhancing drugs on the muscular system | 65 |

1.2.5 Skeletal system

| X | ? | ✓ | Understand the function of the skeletal system for movement, support or protection during physical activity | 68 |

| X | ? | ✓ | Understand the ranges of movement at joints during physical activity | 68 |

| X | ? | ✓ | Understand the effects of regular exercise and physical activity on the skeletal system | 71 |

| X | ? | ✓ | Understand the importance of weight-bearing exercise to prevent osteoporosis | 71 |

| X | ? | ✓ | Understand the potential for skeletal injuries through exercise and physical activity and know common techniques for treatment | 71 |

| X | ? | ✓ | Understand the impact of diet on the skeletal system | 71 |

1.1.1: Healthy, active lifestyles and how they could benefit you

✓ **1.1.1a** Explain what constitutes a healthy, active lifestyle

✓ **1.1.1b** Classify the benefits of a healthy active lifestyle as social, physical or mental

✓ **1.1.1c** Describe the positive effects of physical activity

✓ **1.1.1d** Explain how participation in physical activity can stimulate cooperation, competition, physical challenge, aesthetic appreciation and social mixing

Need more help?
For more on this topic, see pages 10–19 of the main student book (ISBN 978-1-84690-372-4).

edexcel ⊞ key terms

healthy, active lifestyle A lifestyle that contributes positively to physical, mental, and social wellbeing, and includes regular exercise and physical activity.

ResultsPlus
Exam tip

You must know these categories and be able to classify the benefits using them. Remember, aesthetic appreciation is classified as a mental benefit.

ResultsPlus
Exam tip

When students put the correct headings in this table, they usually put the reason or benefit under the correct heading. So remember these headings – physical, social and mental (or psychological) – they could earn you important marks in the exam.

The three areas of benefit to a healthy active lifestyle are:
- physical
- social
- mental.

The reasons for taking part in an activity or sport are shown in the table:

Physical	Social	Mental (or psychological)
• contribute to good physical health • physical challenge • increase fitness • improve performance **Remember** also that any of the health-related exercise terms that you learned will also fit under this heading.	• mix with others • make new friends • meet old/current friends • develop teamwork/ cooperation • work with others **Remember** that social reasons are often easy to spot.	• relieve and/or prevent stress and tension • mental challenge • increase self-esteem and confidence • help the individual feel good • contribute to enjoyment of life • aesthetic appreciation **Remember** these may be the most difficult reasons. They are also known as psychological reasons; you will get a mark if you remember to use the word 'psychological' instead of 'mental'.

Examples of benefits

It is possible to gain all of these benefits (or reasons) from the same activity and at the same time, e.g. by playing team sports like football or hockey, or by taking part in a competition in sports such as golf or gymnastics.

Playing in a competition or team sport can be a **physical** challenge: you will be burning calories, your heart rate will be increasing into the target zone, and you will be improving your levels of fitness, endurance and overall health. Competing is a **mental** challenge, which has the benefits of helping you to forget about other worries in your life and relieving stress. And as part of a team you will be mixing with others, working with others, developing teamwork and cooperation. You will often make friends through playing in a team. These are all **social** benefits.

Aesthetic appreciation can be defined as seeing the beauty in the performance. It can be found in any activity and provides the mental benefit of satisfaction. If you are asked to provide an example of aesthetic appreciation, remember that great unstoppable shot in football that scored a goal, or a diving catch in cricket, or the winning stroke in the Wimbledon final.

Test yourself

1 Which of the following statements best describes a physical benefit of exercise?

   A   Enjoying playing for your team.
   B   Gaining an aesthetic appreciation of movement.
   C   Feeling better about body shape.
   D   Improving body shape.

2 The benefits of taking part in physical activity are listed below.

   a   Write each benefit in the correct column of the table.
   b   Add your own example for each. Each example should be related to a particular sport that you know.

Benefits:

- contribute to enjoyment of life
- contribute to good physical health
- help the individual feel good
- improve performance
- increase fitness
- increase self-esteem and confidence
- make new friends
- mix with others
- meet old/current friends
- mental challenge
- physical challenge
- develop teamwork/cooperation
- relieve and/or prevent stress and tension
- work with others
- aesthetic appreciation

Physical	Social	Mental (or psychological)

ResultsPlus
Watch out!

Remember how to explain aesthetic appreciation. In some past papers the worst answers have been to this question!

ResultsPlus
Build Better Answers

Which of the following best describes a mental benefit of exercise?

A   Meeting new people
B   Losing weight
C   Relieving stress
D   Improved performance

Question 1 is often this type of question. Even if you don't know the answer, you can work it out by a process of elimination. You can rule out **meeting new people**, **losing weight** and **improved performance** so the answer is: **C relieving stress**.

ResultsPlus
Build Better Answers

Possible benefits of taking part in exercise can be grouped as

A   Mental
B   Physical
C   Social
D   Contribute to good physical health

Which of the benefits of exercise named above, A, B, C or D, would best match each of the following statements?

1   I participate in exercise to relieve stress.
2   I joined a local sports club so that I could get out more and meet people.
3   I restarted my training after Christmas to try to lose weight.

In this question, the options have to be matched; once again, this can be done by a process of elimination. Do the obvious ones first. 'Contribute to good physical health' is not a heading, it is a physical benefit. So you can discount it. 'Stress' and 'mental' fit together nicely so **A** matches **1**. 'Meet people' and 'social' fit nicely too so **C** matches **2**. Which leaves **3** to fit with **B**.

So the correct answers are: **1 A, 2 C, 3 B**.

1.1.2: Influences on your healthy, active lifestyle

Need more help?
For more on this topic, see pages 20–29.

ResultsPlus
Exam tip

Key influences are a major part of this topic. There are a lot of questions that could be asked so make sure you know them well.

The six factors are:
1 people
2 image
3 cultural
4 resources
5 health and wellbeing
6 socio-economic.

Influences on taking part

 1.1.2a **Identify key influences on yourself and others in achieving sustained involvement in physical activity**

 1.1.2b **Explain the opportunities available and qualities needed to become or remain involved in physical activity in a range of roles**

You need to know what makes people take part in sport and what encourages them to continue to take part.

In your GCSE PE you have looked at **six** main factors that have an influence on participation.

Each main factor can be broken down into further categories, and you should be able to remember these as well.

1 People

Most people's choice of activity is in some way influenced by others.

(a) Family: a member of your family might introduce you to a sport. Parents who play sport often encourage their children to take part by coming along to their club.

(b) Peers: if your friends play a sport, you might get involved too.

(c) Role models: role models can be anybody whose actions you might copy. They tend to be people you respect, such as your favourite footballer. Having a role model in a particular sport will often mean you want to take part in that activity.

2 Image

All activities have a different image.

(a) Fashion: different activities require different clothing and equipment, and this can sometimes influence what you want to take part in.

(b) Media coverage: a lot of media coverage can make a sport more popular and encourage people to take part.

3 Culture

Sports may appeal to individuals for a number of personal reasons.

(a) Age: some events may have age restrictions. Other sports may appeal to different age groups because of the physical demands or age of the other participants.

(b) Disability: although resources are available for people with disabilities these may be limited in terms of the activities local facilities offer.

(c) Gender: where activities are associated with one gender it can be difficult to get involved if you are of the opposite sex. Activities predominantly played by one gender, or seen in the media as being played by one gender, may appeal more to that gender group.

(d) Race: ethnic background still influences the activities people are involved in, although there are no physiological reasons for this. Once again, this may be a result of media influence.

4 Resources

(a) Access: you must be able to reach a facility if you are to use it. A good location, public transport and car parking all help to make a facility more accessible. Access for those who need ramps, lifts or specialist equipment is also important.

(b) Availability: facilities should be readily available if people are to use them.

(c) Location: it is difficult to reach facilities that are too far away.

(d) Time: facilities need to be open at the right time. For people at work that means in the evening or at weekends and for people at school during school holidays.

5 Health and wellbeing

(a) Illness: individuals who are ill cannot take part.

(b) Health problems: some activities may not be suitable for people with particular health problems, so they have to choose different ones.

It is possible to be 'fit but not healthy'. For example a top athlete who is injured or has a cold will still be fit but is not healthy.

6 Socio-economic

(a) Cost: activities have associated costs such as equipment, hire of facilities or lessons if needed. For example, horse riding costs more than playing football. Being able to afford these costs can often dictate what you can take part in.

(b) Status: this relates to a person's current situation or position in society, e.g. employed, looking for work, or in education. Some sports attract people of a particular status.

ResultsPlus
Build Better Answers

Chloë is a good all-round sports performer and could represent her school in many different sports. Evaluate the potential influence of different factors on Chloë's choice of physical activities. (6 marks)

What are the key word/s in this question? **Evaluate** and **influence**. In this topic there are six headings on the influences on taking part. Choose which to use for your answer. If you base your answer around the **people** heading, **family**, **peers** and **role models** will be the influences to mention.

Remember you will be graded on the quality of your written communication as well as your evaluation of the potential influences.

■ Level 1, 1–2 marks
At this level, answers are brief, making a few simple statements with limited understanding of potential influences on Chloë's choice. The answer might talk about the role model but forget about the influence of peers and family.

● Level 2, 3–4 marks
At this level, answers show some understanding of the influences on Chloë's choice. The answer might talk about specific examples without discussing the category as a whole.

▲ Level 3, 5–6 marks
Answers offer a factually accurate response that shows sound understanding of the influences on Chloë's choice, reflecting a range of examples and explaining the chosen categories.
As there are 6 marks available a good answer would include at least six separate points across a range of categories.

1.1.2c **Explain the sports participation pyramid with regard to the foundation, participation, performance and elite stages**

 1.1.2d **Describe initiatives developed to provide opportunities to become, or remain, involved in physical activity**

Opportunities

As well as taking part in physical activity as a player, you can also become involved in physical activity as a leader, official or volunteer.

- Leadership roles tend to focus on coaching.
- Officials, such as referees and umpires, aim to uphold the rules of a game.
- Many sports and activities, even the Olympic Games, depend on volunteers to help run them.

Initiatives

A number of initiatives have been designed to keep people involved in sport.

1 Government initiatives

A target of two hours physical activity a week was introduced in schools by the government to keep children active.

2 PESSYP (PE, School Sport and Young People)

This initiative aims to strengthen the links between schools and local clubs, making it easier for students to take up physical activity in their spare time and take part in the different roles. This initiative used to be known as PESSCL (PE School Sport Club Links).

3 School Sport Partnerships

School sport partnerships are based around a group of schools with a sports college at the centre, or hub. The aim of the scheme is to develop sporting opportunities in a wide range of sports, and offer high quality coaching and competitions within the local community.

4 Sport England

Sport England creates opportunities for individuals to **start**, **stay** and **succeed** in physical activity.

Start: increase participation in sport in order to improve the health of the nation, with a focus on priority groups.

Stay: retain people in sport through an effective network of clubs, sports facilities, coaches, volunteers and competitive opportunities.

Succeed: create opportunities for talented performers to achieve success.

ResultsPlus
Exam tip

Before going into the examination you should be able to list and explain the different roles that are available in sport. You could even make up a mnemonic to remember the words: **p**layer, **l**eader, **o**fficial and **v**olunteer.

ResultsPlus
Exam tip

Initiatives change over time so keep checking the relevant websites for the most up-to-date information. PESSYP was called PESSCL. You can use either name in your answers.

ResultsPlus
Watch out!

You need to know the definitions of the terms **start**, **stay** and **succeed**.

5 The Youth Sport Trust TOP and Active Kids programme

TOP programmes are designed to encourage people of all abilities to get involved in sport. TOP link for example gives people in the 14—16 age group the chance to organise and manage sports activities. The Active Kids Programme is an example of a voucher programme that schools can use to purchase sporting and other equipment.

For more information on these topics check the official websites. For example:

http://www.youthsporttrust.org/subpage/specialist-sport/index.html

It may be that the influences listed on pages 8—9 encouraged your sporting hero's rise to fame and glory. Take Andy Murray's story, for example:

Andy Murray's mum is a tennis coach (a **leader** and a **volunteer**) and she encouraged Andy and his brother Jamie to play tennis. Andy started to play at the **age** of three and his mother coached him until he was 12. At this point he went to Barcelona to study and play tennis. He lists Muhammed Ali and Ricky Hatton as his sporting **role models**. His brother (**peer**) also plays at a very high level and was mixed doubles champion at Wimbledon. As his mother was a coach he had good access to **facilities**.

To summarise, Andy started playing at a young **age**, had **family** to support him, and had good **access to facilities**. In addition, the sport (tennis) is well covered in the **media** and is **fashionable**, especially during the Wimbledon fortnight. He is sponsored by Fred Perry, manufacturer of his clothes.

In this example, Andy has worked his way up the sports participation pyramid from foundation to elite performer.

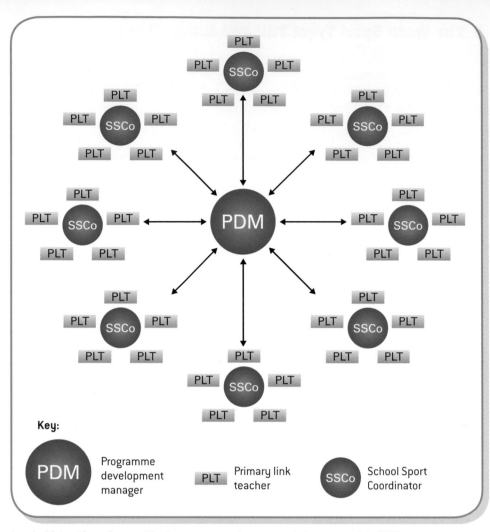

A typical School Sport Partnership cluster. www.teachernet.gov.uk, Crown copyright 2009.

Participation – sports participation pyramid

The sports participation pyramid has four levels:

1   Foundation

The base of the pyramid is where participants learn and experience basic sporting skills, for example in primary school PE lessons or organised activities at the local sports centre. Many people take part at this stage.

2   Participation

Taking part on a more regular basis in a sports programme and being coached, such as on a TOP programme, or belonging to an after-school club or sports club outside school.

3   Performance

Moving up to a higher level with more specialised coaching.

4   Elite/Excellence

The top of the pyramid, moving into representative level at county, regional and national levels. There are fewer people at this level.

ResultsPlus

Exam tip

The pyramid is not a difficult diagram to remember, but you must also remember what each level is called and how it works.

Test yourself

1 Which of the following is a correct statement in relation to Sport England's Start, Stay, Suceed policy?

A Start – increase the number of adults who start their day with exercise

B Start – increase participation in sport in order to improve the health of the nation, with a focus on priority groups

C Stay – aim to keep more officials working in sport so that more people can take part

D Succeed – to win more medals at the Olympic Games

2 The Step into Sport programme aims to provide opportunities for young people to take part in any of four different ways. Being a performer is one. Name the other three.

3 Name and describe the level at the top of the sports participation pyramid.

4 Which of the following is not a government initiative?

A PESSYP

B Active Kids Programme

C Sport England

D The Youth Sport Trust

5 How much time does the government want students to spend on sport in school every week?

1 hour

2 hours

3 hours

4 hours

1.1.3: Exercise and fitness as part of your healthy, active lifestyle

Health, exercise, fitness and performance

 1.1.3a Explain the terms health, fitness and exercise and know how they relate to a balanced, healthy lifestyle and performance in physical activities

Regular **exercise** improves **health** and wellbeing and helps people avoid some health problems, such as obesity. Exercise also helps avoid heart disease, and can relieve stress and tension. The chances of health problems are greater in people who do not exercise.

You can increase your **fitness** levels by **exercising** regularly, which will in turn enhance your **performance**. **Performance** can be affected by your health and fitness.

Need more help?
For more on this topic, see pages 30–43.

edexcel ⠿ key terms

It is important to know these **four** words and how they relate to each other:

exercise A form of physical activity done to maintain or improve health and/or physical fitness. Exercise is not competitive sport.

fitness The ability to meet the demands of the environment.

health A state of complete mental, physical and social wellbeing and not merely the absence of disease and infirmity.

performance How well a task is completed.

ResultsPlus
Exam tip

The definition of health is probably the most difficult to remember. Think of the **three** reasons or benefits of exercise (mental, physical and social) – they are all included in the definition of health.

It does not matter if the three words (physical, social and mental) are in a different order or if you use the word *psychological* instead of the word *mental*.

ResultsPlus
Exam Question Report

Exercise is:
A the ability to meet the demands of the environment
B training regularly
C a state of complete mental, physical and social wellbeing, and not merely the absence of disease and infirmity
D a form of physical activity done primarily to improve one's health and fitness

Answer: D
This type of question often comes up in the multiple choice section. It is one of the easiest question types on the paper so make sure you get it right.
Some students confused the definition of exercise (option D) and fitness (option A above).

(a) What is being described in the statement below? (1 mark)
The ability to meet the demands of the environment.

Answer: Fitness

| | 86% |

Some students confused it with the definition for 'exercise'.

| | 14% |

(b) A gymnast can use many types of equipment such as the rings or a horse. If performers were unable to meet the demands of their environment, what would happen to their performance? (1 mark)

Answer: It would be poor.
A good answer would refer to the performance deteriorating/decreasing/getting worse/falling off/not being able to balance/being poor (or equivalent).

(c) Explain the term performance. (1 mark)

Answer: How well the performer has done.
Some students used 'perform' in their answer and did not get any credit. If you are asked a question 'What is meant by the term performance?', you cannot answer the question by saying it is how well you perform as you have used the word (or part of the word) you have been asked to explain or define.

| | 46% | 0 mark |

Most students answered 'How well the task is completed', which was correct.

| | 54% | 1 mark |

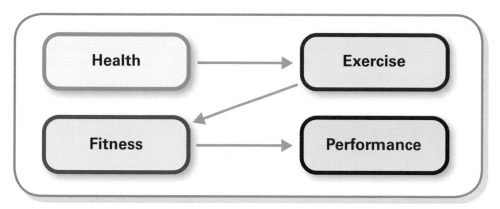

Exercise improves your health, and will also help to improve your fitness.
Improved fitness is one way to improve your performance.

Test yourself

1 Fitness is:

   A   the capability of the heart, blood, blood vessels, lungs and muscles to
   function at optimal efficiency

   B   the ability to meet the demands of the environment

   C   training regularly

   D   a state of complete mental, physical and social wellbeing and not merely
   the absence of disease and infirmity

2 Health is:

   A   the capability of the heart, blood, blood vessels, lungs and muscles to
   function at optimal efficiency

   B   the ability to meet the demands of the environment

   C   a state of complete mental, physical and social wellbeing and not merely
   the absence of disease and infirmity

   D   training regularly

3 Exercise is:

   A   the capability of the heart, blood, blood vessels, lungs and muscles to
   function at optimal efficiency

   B   a form of physical activity done primarily to improve one's health and
   fitness

   C   the ability to meet the demands of the environment

   D   the range of movement possible at a joint

4 What is the definition of performance?

5 Explain how fitness affects performance.

Health-related exercise

 1.1.3b **Know about the components of health-related exercise and relate them to physical activity, identifying their relative importance to different physical activities**

The five components of health-related exercise are:

1 cardiovascular fitness
2 muscular strength
3 muscular endurance
4 flexibility
5 body composition.

You need to know the definitions and be able to give some examples of each.

1 Cardiovascular fitness

This is the most important aspect of health-related exercise. It is important in any long-distance event, e.g. running, swimming, cycling and rowing. It also helps in many team sports such as football, rugby and netball as you are expected to perform over a long period of time.

2 Muscular strength

This is important when a great force is required, e.g. lifting very heavy weights, a gymnast holding a position on the rings, or a rugby player pushing in a scrum.

3 Muscular endurance

Allows muscles to be used repeatedly without getting tired. Muscular endurance is important for long-distance sports such as swimming, running and cycling.

4 Flexibility

Means that the performer can move easily and has a good range of movement in their joints, e.g. swimmers need flexibility in their shoulders to get a good reach in their stroke. Yoga is a good activity to improve flexibility.

5 Body composition

Having the best body shape for your sport. For example, high jumpers are tall and slim which means that their centre of gravity is high, and they are comparatively light in weight so they do not have to get a heavy weight over the bar. Sumo wrestlers are heavy and have a low centre of gravity which makes it difficult to push them over.

 **key terms**

body composition The percentage of body weight that is fat, muscle and bone.
cardiovascular fitness The ability to exercise the entire body for long periods of time.
flexibility The range of movement possible at a joint.
muscular endurance The ability to use the voluntary muscles many times without getting tired
muscular strength The amount of force a muscle can exert against a resistance..

ResultsPlus
Exam tip

In the exam you often need to recall key terms and then apply them to examples of physical activities. There may be more than one correct answer to the first part of the question, but some points will be easier to apply and explain in the second part than others. Make sure that you learn examples of activities to which you can apply the key terms in the exam.

ResultsPlus
Build Better Answers

Using an activity of your choice, state two aspects of health-related exercise (other than flexibility) that may be improved by training. Explain how this would improve performance in your activity. (4 marks)

Activity: Basketball.

Health-related exercise component	How performance is improved
Example: Improved flexibility	Example: Able to stretch further to reach more shots
Student answer: Improved coordination	Student answer: Able to do moves to pass a player.
Student answer: Improved balance	Student answer: Able to defend a player and stay in correct position.

This student recalled skill-related fitness terms rather than health-related exercise so could not possibly get any marks for explaining how this would improve performance in the activity.

A good answer might include:

Health-related exercise component	How performance is improved
Cardiovascular fitness	This would allow him to keep running late in the game and mark his man, and run fast breaks later in the game as well.
Muscular strength	This would make him stronger and so be able to improve performance by allowing him to be stronger to rebound under the back boards at both ends of the court.
Muscular endurance	Would allow him to keep going in driving to the basket later in the game and still be able to jump shoot from outside in the later stages when his muscles would normally be tired.
Body composition	Being tall, and having long arms, would help him intercept and shoot the ball; being tall and slim would also aid in jumping.

ResultsPlus
Exam tip

Choose an activity that you know a lot about if you are allowed to choose an activity to explain. The best way to tackle these questions is to write down all the terms first at the side of the question, or write them on the back of the paper or on a blank page at the start of the examination.

Test yourself

6 For an activity of your choice, explain what each term below means and then give examples of how performance can be improved in this activity by developing each part of fitness.

[*Hint*: choose an activity that is obvious and is easy to apply to the question. You do not get a mark just for writing down the name of the activity – you need to explain which part of the activity.]

Activity: _____

Cardiovascular fitness means: *The ability to exercise the entire body for long periods of time.* Example of how performance is improved in my activity: *Means I can chase down more balls and make returns in tennis.*	Muscular strength means: Example	Muscular endurance means: Example
Flexibility means: Example	Body composition means: Example	

7 Complete the table below. Use a different example for flexibility.

Health-related exercise component	How performance is improved
Example: Improved flexibility	Example: Able to stretch further to reach more shots
Cardiovascular fitness	
Muscular strength	
Muscular endurance	
Flexibility	
Body composition	

Skill-related fitness

 1.1.3c Know about the components of skill-related fitness and relate these to physical activity, identifying their relative importance to different physical activities

The six components of skill-related fitness are:

1 agility
2 balance
3 coordination
4 power
5 reaction time
6 speed.

Agility

This includes changes of both direction and speed. Examples of where agility is needed are:

- in rugby, a player sprinting for the try line will need agility to run fast and change direction to beat an opponent

- in badminton, players not only have to change direction at speed to get to the shuttlecock but also have to decide which shot to use and get into position to return it

- in basketball, a player driving past an opponent to get to the basket will need agility to turn at speed.

A 100 metres sprinter does not need agility – the sprinter runs in a straight line with speed but does not change direction.

Balance

It is important to remember that balance can be static (still) or dynamic (moving). You should know at least one example of each and be able to recognise these in a question and in a picture. A gymnast performing a handstand is holding a static balance but a gymnast moving along a balance beam doing a handspring is using a dynamic (moving) balance. In cricket, a batsman who turns and spins to play a shot must maintain balance to avoid falling on the stumps.

Coordination

At least two body parts must be involved in an action for coordination to be shown. For example, catching a ball involves coordination between hands and eyes; kicking or trapping a football involves coordination between feet and eyes.

Power

You may sometimes have to explain when power is used in the action. This is normally at the moment of impact, e.g.

- when the bat strikes the ball in rounders

- the moment of take off in a jumping event such as high jump

- the moment of take off when jumping to take a rebound in basketball or to spike in volleyball

- the moment of striking the ball in volleyball when spiking.

Reaction time

There must be a trigger (something to set it off), known as the stimulus. The easiest to remember is when the starter fires the gun to start a race (e.g. the 100 metres) and the sprinters are on their starting blocks. Other examples used in questions include games when a player strikes a ball or a shuttlecock and the other player has to react to it. In these examples reacting quickly is essential to success.

Speed

Can be used in sport in many different ways. Speed is demonstrated by a sprinter when running. In tennis, speed is demonstrated by the player getting across the court to return a shot. In hockey, you need speed to get to the ball before your opponent. Speed is demonstrated in any kind of race. You must recognise speed and recall it when you see it and then apply your knowledge when taking on the *explaining* element of the question.

ResultsPlus
Exam tip

Remember that health-related exercise and skill-related fitness are almost always combined to make a great performance. To help you apply your knowledge, watch performances and pick out the aspects of skill-related fitness and health-related exercise that are involved in each one. Try this out on as many different types of activities as possible.

ResultsPlus
Build Better Answers

Coordination is:

A how well a task is completed
B the ability to use two or more body parts together
C the ability to change position quickly and with control
D working together as a team

If you do not recognise B as the definition of coordination, you can still work out the answer. You should quickly see that A is not a skill-related component but is the definition of performance. D relates to the social benefits of taking part in sport. C is the definition of agility (you should recognise this). So the answer must be B.

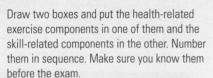

ResultsPlus
Exam tip

Draw two boxes and put the health-related exercise components in one of them and the skill-related components in the other. Number them in sequence. Make sure you know them before the exam.

ResultsPlus
Exam Question Report

A sprinter uses starting blocks at the beginning of a race.
Which of the following components of skill-related fitness are important to a sprinter to get a good start from the blocks?

A Strength
B Coordination
C Body composition
D Reaction time

Answer: D
You can see that two of the options are not skill-related components, so you can narrow the choice down to two possible answers out of four.
Now go for the most obvious answer – do not be tempted to put coordination. It is the start of the race, so the answer is reaction time.

| 91% |

The majority of students were awarded the mark on this question.

| 9% |

Test yourself

8 Fill out the blanks in the paragraph below.

More than one skill can be observed in an activity. A cricketer will not need _____ to run straight down the wicket unless it is necessary to dodge a fielder. Cricketers may need _____ to change position quickly to play a hook shot. They need _____ while moving into position so as to make the shot and not fall and hit their own stumps. They need _____ to see the ball and to play it with the bat. They will need _____ to hit the ball to the boundary (strength in their arms and wrists and speed of the swing of the bat). They need that _____ at the moment that the bat hits the ball. They will need good _____ between seeing the ball released by the bowler (the stimulus) and getting into position to strike the ball. After making a shot they will need _____ to run the 22 yards between the wickets.

9 a Complete the table below by stating how each of the performers will use speed in their performance.

Athlete – sprinter   Games player – hockey   Athlete – discus

	How speed is used in their performance
Athlete – sprinter	
Games player – hockey	
Athlete – discus	

b Coordination is also important to the performers above. Complete the table below by:
  (i) giving an example of the parts of the body being coordinated.
  (ii) explaining how your example of coordination is important to the performers.

	(i) Example of body parts being coordinated	(ii) Explanation of why example of coordination is important to performance
Athlete – sprinter		
Games player		
Athlete – discus		

1.1.4a: Physical activity as part of your healthy, active lifestyle

Health, exercise, fitness and performance

✓ **1.1.4a   Assess personal readiness (PAR-Q)**

✓ **1.1.4b   Assess fitness levels for use in your Personal Exercise Programme**

PAR-Q

Before you start any exercise programme, you need to know that you are ready to do so and that the exercise is suitable.

You can find this out by completing a PAR-Q. A PAR-Q is a questionnaire designed to assess your current state of fitness or your fitness levels.

Typical questions include:

1 Do you have high blood pressure?
2 Do you have increased or high cholesterol?
3 Do you smoke?

Assessing fitness levels

A number of tests are used to assess an individual's health-related exercise and skill-related fitness levels. You need to know the names of the following tests, how they are performed and what they are testing. You also need to know whether they test health-related exercise or skill-related fitness.

In assessing fitness levels, the tests you need to know assess either health-related exercise or skill-related fitness. The trick is to know what you are testing and whether it is a component of health-related exercise or skill-related fitness.

You will almost certainly have used some of these tests before starting on your PEP. This gives you a set of results you can compare your fitness levels with when you have finished, so you can see if you have improved. Testing gives you a benchmark of your fitness levels, so that when you finish your programme you can evaluate it to see if it has improved your fitness levels in the areas you wanted to improve.

Two possible examination questions on this topic could be:

- Why would you use fitness testing? Answer: It is motivational and allows you to set SMART targets.

- When would you use fitness testing? Answer: Before starting a fitness training programme, or at the end.

Need more help?
For more on this topic, see pages 44–79.

edexcel key terms

fitness   The ability to meet the demands of the environment.
PAR-Q   Physical Activity Readiness Questionnaire.
PEP   Personal Exercise Programme.

ResultsPlus
Exam tip

If you are asked in the examination to explain what a PAR-Q is, you need to define what each letter stands for and recall that it is a questionnaire designed to assess an individual's current state of fitness.

Health-related exercise (HRE) tests

Test	Which aspect of HRE does it test?	How do you carry out the test?
Cooper's run	Cardiovascular fitness	Person runs round a measured course for 12 minutes. Work out the distance covered.
Hand grip test	Muscular strength	Person squeezes a hand-grip dynamometer as tightly as possible. Take three measurements and record the best score.
Sit and reach test	Flexibility	Use a standard sit and reach box or sit down with legs straight and feet against a bench on its side. Measure how far beyond the toes the person can reach.

Skill-related fitness (SRF) tests

Test	What aspect of SRF does it test?	How do you carry out the test?
Illinois agility run	Agility	Person lies face down on the floor at the start line. On a signal, the person jumps up and runs around a course which involves many changes of direction. Person completes course as quickly as possible. Run is timed.
Stork stand	Balance	Person stands on both feet, puts hands on hips, lifts leg, putting the foot on the knee of the other leg. When signalled the person raises their heel to stand on tiptoe. Time how long person holds this position. Repeat with other foot. Foot must be kept on the knee.
Sergeant jump	Power	The person chalks their finger-tips and touches the wall as high as possible, stretching their arm above their head. Individual then bends knees and jumps, touching the wall at the highest point of the jump. Measure how high above the standing reach mark they jumped. Record the best of three attempts.
Standing broad jump	Power	Person lies down on the floor and position of feet and head are marked. Person stands at foot marker and jumps as far as they can beyond their own height. Record the best of three attempts.
Ruler drop test	Reaction time	You hold a 1 metre ruler at 0 cm. Person places thumb and forefinger at the 50 cm mark. Person catches the ruler as quickly as possible when you release it. Record the distance from the starting point the person caught the ruler.
30 metres sprint	Speed	Time person sprinting over 30 metres.
3 ball juggle	Coordination	Time how long the person can juggle three tennis balls without dropping one of them or stopping.

ResultsPlus
Watch out!

For the examination you need to know how to conduct the tests (the protocol), for example that in the Illinois Agility run you start from a lying face down position as well as which aspects of HRE or SRF they test.

ResultsPlus
Exam tip

Questions on assessing fitness levels also come up in scenario type questions, which are built around a person. The scenario is called the **stem**. For instance:

James, a 60-year-old male, wants to start an exercise programme after not taking exercise for many years. On his first visit, the fitness instructor advises him about what he needs to do before he can be set an exercise programme.

This is then followed by a **question**:

Give two examples of what James may have been told he should do:

The **answer** might be: an older person may have physical conditions that need to be considered before starting a PEP. Therefore an older person would need to visit a doctor (1), and complete a PAR-Q and physical examination (1), before starting a training programme.

Test yourself

1 Which of the following is the correct meaning of a PAR-Q?

    A a Practical Assessment Readiness Questionnaire

    B a Physical Activity Readiness Questionnaire

    C a Physical Assessment Readiness Questionnaire

    D a Performance Activity Readiness Questionnaire

2 Luke is a national discus champion and uses fitness testing. Give one skill-related fitness factor that he would need for his event and a test that he could use to test this factor.

    [*Hint*: Go for the most obvious skill and then the test that applies to that skill.]

3 Complete the table below.

Test	HRE or SRF	What aspect of SRF or HRE does it test?	How do you carry out the test?
Illinois agility run			Person lies face down on the floor at the start line. When signalled the person jumps up and runs around a course which involves many changes of direction. Person completes course as quickly as possible. Run is timed.
	HRE		Person squeezes a hand-grip dynamometer as tightly as possible. Take three measurements and record the best score.
Sergeant jump		Power	

Revision activity

Go to the internet and search for 'PAR-Q'. Try some of the tests and see if any questions come up in more than one questionnaire, e.g. do you have high blood pressure?

The principles of training

✓ **1.1.4c** Describe, explain and apply the principles of progressive overload, specificity, individual differences/needs, rest and recovery

✓ **1.1.4d** Explain the components of the FITT principle, noting overlap with other principles of training, and how application can lead to improved performance

✓ **1.1.4e** Explain the term 'reversibility', why it might occur and its impact on performance

The principles of training are summarised in this diagram.

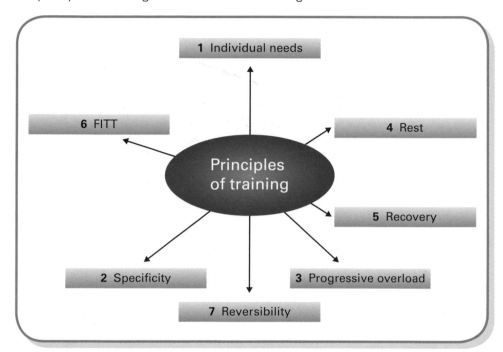

edexcel ⠿ key terms

FITT Frequency, Intensity, Time, Type (used to increase the amount of work the body does in order to achieve overload).
individual needs Matching training to the requirements of an individual.
progressive overload Increasing the amount of overload gradually so that fitness gains occur, but without the potential for injury.
recovery The time required to repair damage to the body caused by training or competition.
rest The period of time allotted to recovery.
reversibility If regular training stops, any adaptation that takes place as a consequence of training will be reversed.
specificity Matching training to the requirements of an activity.

1 Individual needs

The principle of individual differences/needs means matching training programmes to individual requirements. It does not mean matching requirements to a sport. You should consider what you want from your programme and set your targets accordingly.

First, you need to know:
- your current fitness level (fitness testing)
- your sporting experience
- what you hope to achieve (SMART goals).

Then you should consider:
- what you like doing, when and where you can train
- what facilities are available and how much they cost
- whether you prefer to train alone or with a partner or group.

ResultsPlus
Exam tip

Remember, there are seven principles of training.

Once you have answered these questions, you can design a programme to match your requirements. For example, a sprinter taking part in school athletics would not use the same Personal Exercise Programme (PEP) as an Olympic sprinter.

2 Specificity

The principle of specificity means matching training to the requirements of an activity. It is used to design a programme to raise fitness and/or skill levels to improve performance in an individual's particular activity: for example, a sprinter might work on speed, a weight lifter on lifting a heavy weight, and a marathon runner on cardiovascular fitness.

In some sports specificity might apply to training for certain positions. Examples of this could be backs and forwards in rugby, goalkeepers in football and hockey, or shooters in netball.

3 Progressive overload

Progressive overload means gradually increasing the amount of training/work so that an individual gets fitter, without the potential for injury. As your fitness increases, you can gradually make the training harder. This can be done by increasing the intensity in each different training method.

The speed and level of progressive overload will vary according to the person doing the training. Someone starting out on a new programme will progress more slowly and may not reach the intensity of a professional or indeed a person who has been training over a longer period of time. Once a reasonable level of fitness has been established, they might work more intensely in some sessions in order to raise their level of fitness.

4 Rest

You cannot exercise and train continually without taking some rest as this may lead to injury. Exercise and training damage your muscles and body, which need time to recover and rebuild before further training. Rest is the time allotted to recovery to allow adaptations to take place before further training.

5 Recovery

Recovery is the time required to repair damage to the body caused by training or competition. The body adapts to the hard training and builds itself back up again.

ResultsPlus

Exam tip

The principle is called specificity and this is the word you must use in the examination. Specific, specify and specification are not correct; students who used these terms in previous papers received no marks.

ResultsPlus

Exam tip

To use the principle of progressive overload, training must be increased gradually. A training programme that changes from three 20 minute sessions a week (total one hour per week) to four 30 minute sessions a week (total two hours) is not progressive, as there is not a gradual increase.
For progressive overload, it would be sensible to increase each session by 10 minutes for at least two weeks before adding the extra session, or add an extra session for two weeks before increasing the lengths of the sessions two by two.

6 The FITT Principle

This principle has four aspects, each of which needs to be considered whatever the programme.

F   is for frequency, and relates to how often you train.

I   is for intensity and relates to how hard you train. This can be measured to some extent by working in the target zone (that is between 60 to 80 per cent of your maximum heart rate).

> You must know how to change the intensity you are exercising at depending on the method of training you are using. For example, if you are using weight training, you can increase intensity by lifting a heavier weight or doing more repetitions. Increasing intensity in interval training would mean running faster or taking shorter rest intervals, in continuous training running a longer distance, and in fartlek running up a steeper hill or running faster up the same hill.

T   is for time and relates to how long your training sessions last. A minimum of 20 minutes is recommended for general fitness. Remember that this is the actual training period with your heart rate in the target zone.

T   is for the type or method of training you intend to do (this will be covered later) and this will again depend on what you want from your training. For example, cardiovascular fitness can be gained from a wide variety of activities as long as your heart rate is raised for long enough and to a high enough intensity.

7 Reversibility

If an individual stops training, any adaptation that has occurred as a result of training, such as increased fitness, will be lost or 'reversed'. You do not want to apply this principle. Less training, less intensity, missed training sessions, injury and illness are all causes of this final principle of reversibility.

Summarising the FITT principle

What do the letters stand for?

- F stands for frequency – how often you train, minimum recommended is three times a week.

- I stands for intensity or how hard you train (similar to progressive overload).

- T stands for time or how long your heart rate is in the target zone (see 1.1.4c pages 36–39).

- T stands for type or method of training (see 1.1.4b pages 32–35).

ResultsPlus
Exam tip

It is important to know what each letter stands for in the FITT principle as this is sometimes tested in the multiple choice questions.

ResultsPlus
Exam tip

Remember you cannot improve fitness by using the principle of reversibility; reversibility will mean a drop or fall in fitness levels due to inactivity.

1.1.4b: Physical activity as part of your healthy, active lifestyle

Methods of training

 1.1.4h **Describe a range of methods of training and explain how these can improve health and fitness, and their relationships with the components of fitness**

 1.1.4i **Link methods of training to specific physical activities based on the associated health-related exercise and skill-related fitness requirements**

The best way to learn methods of training is through experience. If you have performed a PEP you will probably have experienced at least some of them. You need to know about six for your examination. They are:

1   interval training
2   continuous training
3   fartlek training
4   circuit training
5   weight training
6   cross training.

Interval training

Interval training can be defined as periods of hard work followed by periods of rest.

The periods of work could be sprinting 80 metres at 90–100 per cent of maximum effort/speed, followed by resting to allow recovery so that further repetitions of high intensity/hard work can be performed.

The athlete may perform six repetitions to make one set, then rest for ten minutes; perform a second set followed by another ten minutes rest; then perform a third set; totalling three sets of ten repetitions.

Advantages of interval training

The working period of interval training improves speed and strength and the rest period allows recovery, so a person performing interval training is always working at a high intensity, as in the FITT principle.

Who uses it?

Sprinters are the most obvious choice. They could be sprinters on the track, or swimmers in the pool. Any athlete who needs high speed would use interval training. Performers who need anaerobic fitness also rely on interval training.

Different sports use interval training in different ways.

- **Interval training for individual sports**
  In swimming, you may be required to start a two-length swim when the pool clock is at the top of the minute and then start another two-length swim when it reaches the top of the minute again. The quicker you swim your two lengths the longer the rest you get.

- **Interval training for racket games**
  In racket games, you may be required to retrieve a shot from the forehand court followed quickly by one from the backhand court for ten successive forehands and backhands.

Continuous training

As the name implies, this means continuous exercise usually at a moderate to slow pace; there are no rest periods. The intensity is lower and the heart rate will not be so high during this type of training (the I in the FITT principle of training).

Advantages of continuous training

Athletes primarily use continuous training to improve cardiovascular and aerobic fitness. Continuous training often means running, but other suitable activities include swimming, cycling and using a rowing machine, stepper or cross trainer.

Who uses it?

Endurance athletes in any sport, such as running, swimming, cycling and rowing, use continuous training. It can also be used by some games players, especially as preparation at the start of the season.

Fartlek training

The term comes from the Swedish word for 'speedplay'. Fartlek training combines high and low intensity work, such as running fast/sprinting and jogging, and different terrain, such as hills, forest and sand dunes.

Advantages of fartlek training

It is used to improve speed and endurance.

Who uses it?

Fartlek training matches the type of fitness that many games players need because it includes the short bursts of activity – such as starting, stopping and sprinting – typical of games such as rugby, football, netball and hockey.

Circuit training

Circuit training combines a variety of exercises or skills into a circuit, normally arranged in a gym or sports hall. In a fitness circuit, participants complete exercises, for example as many press-ups as they can manage in 30 seconds, followed by a brief rest while they move to another exercise station. Stations are arranged in a specific order so that the same muscle group is not exercised twice in a row. After completing the first circuit, participants may rest for three minutes before performing a second and then a third circuit.

Advantages of circuit training

Circuit training improves general fitness, cardiovascular fitness and muscular endurance. Other advantages include:
* not much equipment is necessary
* therefore it is relatively inexpensive
* can be done at home or in a gym
* participants can work alone or with others
* a large area is not needed
* music can be used for motivation.

Who uses it?

Games players and swimmers often use it because they need all round fitness.

ResultsPlus
Exam tip

Make sure you understand that, although fartlek training is similar to interval training, it is not the same. If asked to compare fartlek and interval training, remember that fartlek includes sprints over varying distances, unlike interval training where distances are measured, and fartlek training takes place over a variety of terrain.

ResultsPlus
Exam tip

To help you remember the six methods of training, think of all the c's first (circuit, continuous, cross) and then the other three (weight, internal, fartlek).

A **station** is the place where you do the exercise.

A **repetition** is one exercise, for example one press-up.

A **set** is the number of repetitions you plan to perform or the amount you can do in a set amount of time.

A **circuit** is one lap of all the exercises.

A skills circuit is similar to a fitness circuit but has skill stations instead of fitness exercise stations. A skills circuit in netball, for example, would include catching, passing, and shooting.

Weight training

Weight training is sometimes called resistance training. In weight training the resistance is normally a weight on either a machine or free weights or a barbell or dumbbells. Unlike circuit training, one set of repetitions of a particular exercise follows another after a short rest. In weight training, you perform three sets of the same exercise before moving on.

Advantages of weight training

Heavy weights improve muscular strength. Lighter weights with more repetitions improve muscular endurance.

Who uses it?

Athletes, swimmers, games players and others all use weight training, using the principle of individual needs to match the programme to the individual. It is also a popular method of training for people who just want to get fit.

Cross training

Cross training is a combination of any of the other methods of training.

Advantages of cross training?

Cross training is used because most people need a combination of types of fitness. Cardiovascular fitness and muscular endurance are probably the most common combination.

Who uses it?

Almost everyone who wants to get fit, as well as nearly every sports performer, uses cross training as it can easily be adapted to suit individual needs. Games players need speed so interval training is very important, but they also need cardiovascular fitness which some continuous and/or fartlek training can help them to achieve. At the same time, they might want to build up their muscular strength. All these things can be achieved by setting out a cross training programme which combines the most suitable methods of training.

Method	Why?	Who?	Example
Circuit training	All round fitness	Games players	Badminton
Continuous	Cardiovascular fitness/muscular endurance	Distance runners/ swimmers/cyclists	Marathon
Interval	Speed	Sprinters	Athletics/swimming
Weight	Strength	Athletes	Sprinting
Fartlek	Speed	Games players	Football/netball
Cross	Combination of other methods	Most sports	Athletics/swimming

Remember that the methods of training can be linked back to the benefits and reasons for taking part. All three main benefits of exercise can be gained through using these training methods.

- They can help people to lead a healthy, active lifestyle and gain many of the benefits outlined in Topic 1.1.1. All the physical benefits, including the aspects of health-related exercise and the components of skill-related fitness, can be gained by following a PEP which uses these methods to improve, for example, cardiovascular fitness and muscular endurance. The methods of training also provide a physical challenge in every exercise session.

- Using the methods of training has mental (psychological) benefits, such as increasing individual wellbeing and relieving stress and tension. This is because exercise produces serotonin, the 'feel good hormone'.

- People usually exercise and train with others, so training becomes a social activity.

Test yourself

1 Insert the appropriate words in the spaces below to suit the profile outlined and complete the scenario. Some are added at the start to give you the idea of what is required. The example words are in bold italics.

Albert is aged 92 and runs each year in the London Marathon. His training consists of a **_continuous_** training programme that is mostly **_jogging_**, but could also include _____ or _____.

Matt represents his county at the All England Schools Athletics Championships in the 400 metres so he needs to improve his _____ fitness. In order to do this he uses _____ training. This type of training includes periods of _____ at a high _____ followed by periods of _____.

Another type of training that might produce a similar effect on the individual is called _____, which means _____. This type of training can involve _____ running which will again increase the _____ and so raise the heart rate.

Luke is a national under-20 throwing champion so he does not use this type of training. Instead, in his winter training programme, he uses _____ training for general fitness and muscular _____. This is very useful for him because it is _____, which helps because he is on a student grant. He can also work with his friends who may be of _____ abilities but their programme will suit their _____ _____, another important _____ of training. In this type of training, the exercises are arranged so that they suit the particular athlete and so fulfil the _____ of _____.

Finally, there is Gary, the footballer, who needs a _____ of the two types of fitness so in his training programme he will include both. Other sports also require a combination of training methods.

1.1.4c: Physical activity as part of your healthy, active lifestyle

The exercise session

✓ 1.1.4j Plan and present examples from typical exercise sessions to match the fitness requirements of selected physical activities or individuals

✓ 1.1.4k Understand the exercise session and the purpose of each component

✓ 1.1.4l Explain the use of the principles of training within an exercise programme, showing how they may be applied in planning to improve health and fitness as part of a healthy lifestyle

✓ 1.1.4m Link methods of training to aerobic and anaerobic activity

The exercise session, competition or match/game is split into three phases:
1 warm-up   2   main activity   3   cool-down.

The warm-up

The warm-up is also split into three phases. In examination questions the first two do not usually cause students much of a problem.

1 **Pulse raising activity** Reason: to prepare the heart for the task ahead by raising the heart rate near to what it will be when the main activity or competition starts. How you do this will be related to what the activity is: e.g. jogging if the activity is running, swimming if the activity is swimming, cycling if the activity is cycling, and so on.

2 **Stretching** Reason: to avoid injury by taking the muscles and joints through the range of motion that will be used during the main activity.

3 **Specific skill-related practice** Reason: to practice performing skills related to the activity. Tennis players will practice their tennis shots and service, bowlers their run up. If it is a game that involves running fast then the first sprint should be in the warm-up, not the game. This is the area where many students lose marks either because they leave it out altogether, do not know what it is or do not use a suitable activity.

The main activity

This could be a competition, for instance a football or netball match, or an exercise session designed to meet the individual's specific needs – for example, interval training for speed or continuous training for endurance.

The cool-down

Like the warm-up, the cool-down can be split into three parts.

1 A similar activity to **pulse raising**, this time to bring the heart rate gradually back to its normal or resting speed.

2 **Stretching** to disperse lactic acid which builds up in muscles during activity.

3 Some **relaxation** may be used to relieve stress and tension after a hard exercise session or match.

edexcel ⠿ key terms

aerobic With oxygen. If exercise is not too fast and is steady, the heart can supply all the oxygen muscles need.
anaerobic Without oxygen. If exercise is done in short, fast bursts, the heart cannot supply blood and oxygen to muscles as quickly as the cells use them.

ResultsPlus
Exam tip

Your PEP is a good revision tool for many of the topics, including the exercise session. Look at your PEP. Make sure that you can recall each point you need to know and explain how to apply it.

Aerobic and anaerobic activity

One of the important things to remember about exercise and sporting activities is that they are related to anatomy and physiology and have different requirements.

- **Anaerobic activity** occurs in sports that rely almost entirely on speed, for example a 100 metre sprint. A sprinter's training and training methods will be designed to improve this.

- **Aerobic activity** relies predominantly on cardiovascular fitness. It occurs in sports such as long distance running. Long distance runners need to be able to work the whole body for long periods of time.

- Many games require a combination of both types of fitness. Footballers, tennis players and hockey players need both to be quick and to be able to play over a long period of time. They have to train to improve both aerobic and anaerobic fitness.

To sum up, long distance runners do not run out of breath when they run a marathon unless they have to sprint to the finish line to win, so they work **aerobically**, or with oxygen. Sprinters, especially the 400 metres runners, do run out of breath so work **anaerobically**, or without oxygen.

Results Plus
Exam tip

Many students think that the cool-down can help to prevent injury. This is wrong; the cool-down takes place after the event, so cannot prevent an injury.

Test yourself

A warm-up is a very important part of preparation before competition.

1 State **three** reasons why a warm-up is thought to be good preparation before a competition.

2 A warm-up is a very important part of a sprinter's preparation before the race. Complete the table below. State the phases of the warm-up and describe a typical activity for each phase.

Phase of warm-up	Typical activity

3 Which of the following is a benefit of a cool-down?
- A Reduces the chance of injury during activity.
- B Increases blood flow around the body.
- C Increases the production of lactic acid.
- D Reduces the risk of muscle stiffness after exercise.

4 At the end of a marathon, with 385 yards to go, three runners are very close together. They sprint for the finish.
- a At this point, are the performers working aerobically or anaerobically?
- b In the previous 26 miles, were they working aerobically or anaerobically?
- c Explain your answers.

Analysing training sessions

 1.1.4n **Understand what is meant by resting heart rate, working heart rate and recovery rates, plot examples on a graph and evaluate results**

 1.1.4o **Use graphs to demonstrate and explain the use of target zones and training thresholds**

Heart rates

When people train, their **heart rate** (the number of times the heart beats per minute) is affected. One of the first indications or immediate effects of taking part is that the heart beats faster: this is known as the **working heart rate**.

Resting heart rate (the number of times a heart beats at rest) is recognised as a good measure of a person's fitness. A low resting heart rate indicates a good fitness level, and a high resting heart rate indicates a low fitness level.

Heart recovery rate (the time it takes for the heart to return to its resting rate after stopping exercise) is also a good indicator of fitness. The faster a person's working heart rate returns to normal, the fitter the individual.

The thresholds of training and target zone

Using the **thresholds of training** gives a good indication of how hard you are training. These indicate the target zone you are aiming for your heart to be in when you are training.

Thresholds of training can be calculated using a simple equation. The formula is:

220 minus your age, multiplied by 60 per cent gives you the lower threshold of training.

220 minus your age, multiplied by 80 per cent gives you the upper threshold of training.

The **target zone** lies between these thresholds and is where you should be aiming in your training session. The higher into the target zone the higher the intensity of the exercise session (from the FITT principle).

Analysing different types of training sessions

In the following graphs the red and blue lines show the thresholds of training, here set at 123 and 164 beats per minute for someone aged 15. The heart rate is represented by the black line. For the examination you should be able to determine which method of training is being shown in each graph.

The heart rates will vary according to the method of training being used.

Remember the formula:
220 – your age × 60 per cent, and × 80 per cent gives you the thresholds of training and your target zone.
If you are 16, the target zone is between 123–164 beats per minute. Remember it is beats **per minute**.

Here the individual has worked hard for a short time at a high intensity and the heart rate has increased, in some cases exceeding the upper threshold. The individual then rests and their heart rate comes back down. The intervals are regular as you would expect in interval training.

Interval training

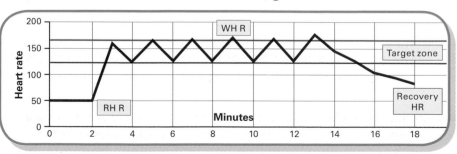

Continuous training

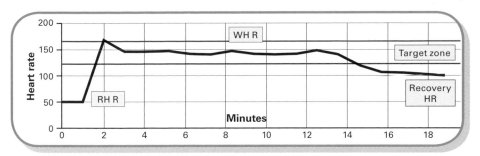

In this graph the heart rate has increased when the individual started to train and then stayed at quite a constant level. This indicates a continuous level of training (perhaps going up a little for example if there is a hill to climb), which is an indication of continuous training.

Fartlek training

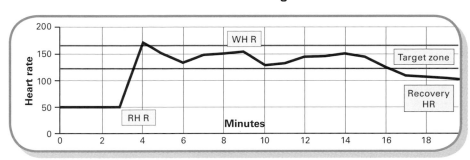

This graph shows an irregular heart rate pattern, indicating work at quite a high intensity followed by lower intensity and so on. The work does not follow a regular pattern as you would find in interval training, therefore this is what you would find in fartlek training.

Circuit training

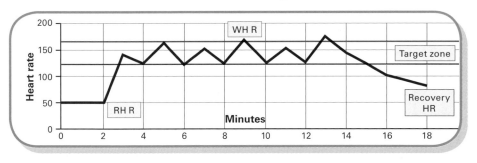

In this graph, high intensity work is followed by lower intensity work in a regular pattern. As the heart rate changes, this would indicate circuit training, where some of the exercises are harder than others, varying the intensity of the heart rate.

In addition to reading the intensity of the heart rate during work, it is important to be able to observe when the student's heart rate went into and came out of the target zone, so that you can calculate how long their heart rate was in the target zone. You should also be able to calculate how long it took for the student's heart to return to its resting rate at the end of the training session – the recovery rate.

Comparing two types of training session

People train for different reasons, they gain different benefits and use different training methods. A graph of a person's heart rate during a training session reveals a lot. This is an area where you need to apply all the aspects of the course you have studied and revised.

While performing this task you can revise many aspects of the course: start by recalling what you have gone over and revised already. Then you can show your understanding and ability to apply this knowledge by explaining what has happened in these exercise sessions.

The examination always includes questions built around a scenario or a short story, which is known as the stem of the question. This is not the actual question but the information on which the question is based. It may also include a picture, a table or, as in the example which follows, a graph; you need to get information from the graph to answer the questions.

Results**Plus**
Exam tip

If you did this activity when performing your PEP you could read over your information and evaluate it as part of your revision.

Test yourself

Carl and Zoe are both in Year 11 and are very good athletes. They run for their school and for their athletics club and both have been selected to represent their county in the National Schools Championships.

They have trained hard for some time and at their last training session their coaches got them to wear heart rate monitors to monitor and record their heart rates so that their training could be analysed. The resulting graphs are shown below; use them to help you to answer the questions below.

Zoe runs the 3000 metres and Carl runs the 100 metres.

Athlete A

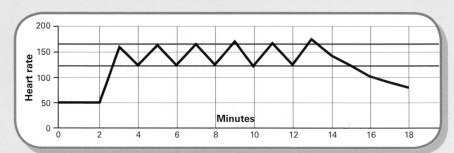

Athlete B

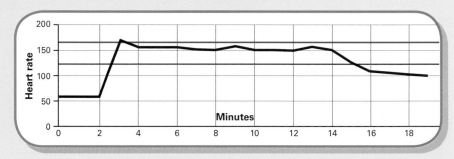

5 From the information you have been given about Carl and Zoe, decide which is athlete A and which is athlete B.

6 **a** What training method is athlete A is using?
  b Explain your answer.
  c What is this method used to improve?
  d Is this health-related exercise or skill-related fitness?
  e If the athlete was training to improve this particular aspect of fitness which principle of training would they be applying?

7 **a** What training method is athlete B using?
  b Explain your answer.
  c What is this method used to improve?
  d Is this health-related exercise or skill-related fitness?
  e Is this method of training aerobic or anaerobic?
  f Explain your answer.

Test yourself

8 What are the horizontal red and blue lines indicating on the graphs?

9 Explain how the position of these lines is calculated.

10 What is the name given to the area within these two lines?

11 How long did Athlete A train with their heart rate in this area?

12 How long did Athlete B train with their heart rate in this area?

13 Which part of the FITT principle does this apply to?

14 a The two athletes train four times a week. Which part of the FITT principle does this apply to?

   b If they train four times a week they have three days off. Which two principles of training does this apply to?

15 There are points in the first graph where the heart rate goes higher and then comes back down again. Which aspect of the FITT principle does this apply to?

16 Does Carl or Zoe have the lower resting heart rate? What is it?

17 Explain Carl and Zoe's working heart rate in relation to each other's graph.

18 After evaluating their training programmes the coaches decide it is time to move the two athletes on in their training. Which principle of training will they apply to do this?

19 If the coaches decide to let Carl and Zoe do some weight training, which aspect of health-related exercise will Carl be working on and which aspect will Zoe be working on?

20 The two athletes are now using more than one training method – which method of training is this?

21 The coaches plan a programme for Carl and a different programme for Zoe. Which principle of training are they applying?

22 The coaches will plan three parts in each exercise session. The first part will be the warm-up. Name the other two.

23 The warm-up is the first part of the training session. Name the three parts of a warm-up.

24 Give two reasons why an athlete should perform a warm-up.

1.1.5: Your personal health and wellbeing

The exercise session

✓ 1.1.5a **Understand the link between exercise, diet, work and rest, and their influence on personal health and wellbeing**

✓ 1.1.5b **Explain the requirements of a balanced diet**

✓ 1.1.5c **Explain the importance and uses of macro and micro nutrients, carbohydrates, proteins, fats, vitamins, minerals, water and fibre in maintaining a healthy, active lifestyle**

✓ 1.1.5d **Explain the need to consider the timing of dietary intake when performing due to the redistribution of blood flow during exercise**

A balanced diet

A balanced lifestyle carefully combines exercise, diet, work and rest so that the individual feels good and maintains their wellbeing. In this equation diet plays an important role, as it provides all the nutrients for health, fitness and wellbeing.

A balanced diet provides the energy to work, exercise, and rest and repair tissues. It also maintains an energy balance:

calories in = calories out

Active people, such as footballers, use more energy and therefore need more calories and more of the foods that provide them. Individuals who live a sedentary lifestyle (one that does not involve much physical activity) and eat more calories than they use tend to put on weight.

As you have seen, energy balance depends on calories in being equal to calories out. If you stop exercising for any reason, through injury for example, it is important to keep a balance between the amount of calories taken in and the amount of calories used up so that you neither lose nor gain weight. This is known as energy balance.

Factors of a balanced diet

There are seven factors of a balanced diet and these are split into two smaller parts.

Macro nutrients

Macro nutrients form the biggest part of what we eat.

Carbohydrates and **fat** provide us with most of the energy we need to exercise, do our work and enjoy our social life.

Protein is used to build and repair muscle.

There are two types of carbohydrates, shown in the table on the right.

Simple: sugars	Sources include: biscuits cakes chocolate fruit vegetables
Complex: starch	Found in natural foods. Sources include: brown rice wholemeal bread potatoes pasta bananas

Need more help? For more on this topic, see pages 80–91.

edexcel ▦ key terms

balanced diet A diet which contains an optimal ration of nutrients.
macro nutrients Carbohydrate; protein; fat.
micro nutrients Vitamins and minerals; water; fibre.

Most of our energy should come from carbohydrates. This type of energy is stored in our muscles and liver as glycogen. It can be quickly converted into glucose and provides us with energy.

Fats

Although most of our energy should come from carbohydrates, fats also provide energy. This can come from butter, margarine and cooking oil as well as from meat and cheese. We burn energy from fat when we exercise over long periods of time so if we want to burn fat we need to exercise for longer at a lower intensity.

Protein

Protein is particularly important for building and repairing muscle tissue. Muscles are damaged during exercise, for example when lifting weights. It is important to use the principles of rest to allow our muscles to repair, recover and adapt so that they are stronger when we exercise the next time. It can also provide energy when we exercise over very long periods of time, such as in a marathon race.

Micro nutrients

Micro nutrients are needed in smaller quantities than macro nutrients.

Vitamins

Vitamins are essential but are only needed in small amounts. They can be found in dairy products, fresh vegetables, meat, cereals, nuts, fruit and vegetable oil, and they help our vision, skin, bones, teeth and healing capability, among other things. A balanced diet should provide all the vitamins you need, although some people take vitamins in tablet form.

Minerals

There are many minerals that need to be included in a balanced diet and they all have a particular function. **Calcium** and **iron** are two of the most important. They are mentioned here because they also appear in a different context in other parts of the course. It is therefore important to understand why they are necessary for everyone, as well as how they meet the specialist needs of sports people and athletes.

> **Calcium** is vital to health, especially during growth in childhood and adolescence. It is important in the formation of bones and teeth, and helps to make the bones strong. It is also important for older people as it helps to maintain bone density which decreases with age.

> **Iron** is essential because it is involved in the formation of red blood cells and is also important to haemoglobin and the oxygen carrying capacity of the blood. Without iron, the blood would not be able to carry oxygen around the body. It is especially important for athletes involved in distance events.

Water

Water holds oxygen and is the main component of many cells. It transports nutrients, waste and hormones around the body and controls the distribution of electrolytes (body salts). It is essential to control body temperature. During exercise, the body sweats, and without water becomes dehydrated. In sport this often happens, especially in the longer endurance events and activities, such as the Tour de France, the London Marathon and long boxing matches, where the athletes and performers sweat profusely.

ResultsPlus
Exam tip

There are three macro elements (carbohydrate, protein and fat) and two micro nutrients (vitamins and minerals). You need to know the importance and use of each.
You also need to understand the importance of a balanced **diet** and how it affects our ability to **exercise** and **work**, e.g. **the use of carbohydrates to provide us with energy** and the importance of **rest** together with a good **protein** intake in order to recover, repair and build our bodies.

Fibre

Wholegrain cereals and bread provide insoluble fibre that bulks our food and helps to prevent constipation. Fruit and vegetables provide soluble fibre that helps to reduce blood cholesterol levels, another area you need to know about and will revise later.

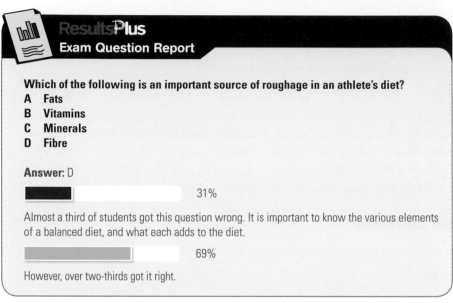

ResultsPlus
Exam Question Report

Which of the following is an important source of roughage in an athlete's diet?
A   Fats
B   Vitamins
C   Minerals
D   Fibre

Answer: D

31%

Almost a third of students got this question wrong. It is important to know the various elements of a balanced diet, and what each adds to the diet.

69%

However, over two-thirds got it right.

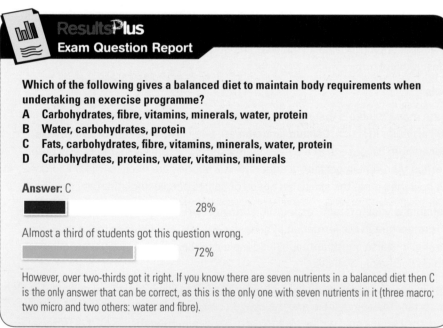

ResultsPlus
Exam Question Report

Which of the following gives a balanced diet to maintain body requirements when undertaking an exercise programme?
A   Carbohydrates, fibre, vitamins, minerals, water, protein
B   Water, carbohydrates, protein
C   Fats, carbohydrates, fibre, vitamins, minerals, water, protein
D   Carbohydrates, proteins, water, vitamins, minerals

Answer: C

28%

Almost a third of students got this question wrong.

72%

However, over two-thirds got it right. If you know there are seven nutrients in a balanced diet then C is the only answer that can be correct, as this is the only one with seven nutrients in it (three macro; two micro and two others: water and fibre).

Dietary intake and performance

Knowing what to eat is important so that you can ensure that you have a balanced diet. It is also important to eat at the proper times in relation to when you intend to exercise or compete.

When we eat we need blood to be directed to the digestive system to help to digest the food. The blood flow is increased to the digestive system by widening the blood vessels, whilst blood flow to other areas of the body is reduced by constriction.

When we exercise or compete blood needs to be pumped to our working muscles to provide the oxygen they need to keep them going. This is known as **blood shunting**.

If we eat just before exercising or competing, the blood will be pumped to our muscles and so will not be available in the gut for digestion, which might cause us to have stomach cramps.

It is therefore important to eat at least two to three hours before you intend to exercise so that the food will be digested to provide energy and blood will be available to deliver much-needed oxygen to the working muscles.

Summary

- Eat a light meal high in carbohydrate at least two hours before training or competing.

- Understand the energy requirements for your sport and know where the energy in your diet comes from.

- Remember to drink plenty of water and fruit juice especially if you exercise or take part in sport.

- Try to avoid unsaturated fats and limit animal fats as these are high in cholesterol.

Test yourself

1 Name both types of carbohydrate (other than simple and complex).

2 Norbert likes chocolate and cake, which form of carbohydrate is this?

3 Luke is a discus thrower. For his event he would emphasise one of the macro nutrients in his diet. Which would it be?

4 If people are conscious of their weight which of the macro nutrients should they cut down on to lose weight?

5 Calcium is an important mineral. Give one example of why it is important.

6 Why should a marathon runner drink plenty of water during a race?

7 When we exercise, blood is sent to the working muscles. This means that less blood is available for digesting food, which is why we should not eat too close to exercise. What is this process known as?

1.2.1: Physical activity and your healthy mind and body

 1.2.1a **Describe the different body types and explain the effect of each on participation and performance**

Somatotypes

There are three basic body types, or somatotypes. The picture below will help you to build an image of each of these in your mind. In fact, most people's bodies are a combination of somatotypes; the optimum body type for a particular sport is often a mixture of two somatotypes.

- **Endomorph** – short/dumpy with narrow shoulders and broad hips, pear shaped with a low centre of gravity. Extra weight means that endomorphs tend to be less mobile, therefore less likely to excel at sports requiring speed.

- **Mesomorph** – broad shoulders with narrow hips; muscular. Mesomorphs are often good at sports and activities that require power or strength.

- **Ectomorph** – low body weight, tall and thin with a high centre of gravity. Ectomorphs often take part in endurance activities.

These are extreme examples of the three somatotypes.

Endomorphs and sport

- Endomorphs often excel in sports requiring strength but not stamina, as they will usually have extra weight to carry.

- The most obvious sport which requires participants to be heavy is sumo wrestling. As the contests usually last a very short time, lack of endurance does not matter as much as in other sports.

Mesomorphs in sport

- Mesomorphs can usually perform well in a wide variety of sports, especially those requiring strength, speed and the combination of these two factors, power.

- These somatotypes dominate traditional sports such as sprinting, swimming and rowing. Male gymnasts are often mesomorphs. This body type can also be found in positions in games such as scrum half and fly half in rugby, where their speed, strength and agility are important.

Need more help?

For more on this topic, see pages 94–113 of the main student book (ISBN 978-1-8490-372-4).

edexcel key terms

ectomorph An individual with narrow shoulders and narrow hips, a somatotype characterised by thinness.

endomorph An individual with wide hips and narrow shoulders, a somatotype characterised by fatness.

mesomorph An individual with wide shoulders and narrow hips, a somatotype characterised by muscularity.

somatotype Classification of body type.

ResultsPlus Exam tip

It is very important to know the three different body types, endomorph, mesomorph and ectomorph, what sporting activities these body types are most suitable for and where they appear in top sporting activities, e.g. in the Olympic Games, mesomorphs will be found in the sprint events and ectomorphs in the marathon.

ResultsPlus Exam tip

In the examination you may be asked to explain why a body type is advantageous for a certain sport. To be awarded the mark you must give a reason rather than a simple explanation. For example, if you said that a high jumper carries less weight and can therefore jump higher you would be awarded a mark. If you just said that a high jumper weighs less, you would not.

Ectomorphs in sport

- Ectomorphs have the opposite body type to endomorphs and can often be found in endurance events. It is sometimes said that the longer the race, the thinner the athlete.

- Other sports that suit ectomorphs are high jump, where their height, low weight and higher centre of gravity makes it easier for them to jump high, and horse racing, where jockeys need to be small and light so the horse has less weight to carry.

Results Plus
Exam Question Report

Complete the table below.
(i) Name the body type of each performer in the table. (3 marks)
(ii) State one reason why this body type is an advantage to the performer mentioned in the table in his/her sport. (3 marks)

Performer	(i) Body type	(ii) Reason for advantage
sprinter		
tennis player		
high jumper		

Answer:
e.g. (i)   sprinter – mesomorph
      (ii) is able to run faster as has more strength, and therefore more power.

■ Over 25 per cent of students failed to get any marks. Some students said that a high jumper is lighter, but then lost marks because they did not explain the advantage.

● Most students scored well when identifying the associated body type with the sports performer. Students found it more difficult to give an advantage for the individual's body type that was specific to their sport.

▲ A good answer would give three reasons that are specific to their chosen sport, for example, the high jumper having less weight means that they can achieve greater heights with less resistance.

Test yourself

1 The term body type is one way of expressing the body build of a person but what is the technical term used to describe body type?

2 From the list of sports given to the right indicate which somatotype you think would be most fitting for each. You could use a combination of somatotypes for some of them.

3 Identify the somatotypes of the athletes shown below.

Sport/activity
tennis/Wimbledon
100m sprint/Olympic final
flat racing (jockey)
football/midfield player
basketball/rebounder
bodybuilding/World's Strongest Man
sumo wrestling

Optimum weight

 1.1.2b Outline why and how expected and optimum weight varies according to height, gender, bone structure and muscle girth; explain how this may affect participation and performance in physical activity

 1.1.2c Explain the terms anorexic, obese, overfat, overweight, underweight; explain how they may impact on achieving a sustained involvement in physical activity

Your optimum weight is the best weight for you. Optimum weight is different for different people; it varies according to several factors which are described below. Doctors sometimes use the Body Mass Index (BMI), which takes into account gender and height, to assess weight.

Factors affecting weight

Gender

A man who is 5'6" tall is likely to be heavier than a woman of the same height, because men tend to have more muscle and larger bones. Therefore their acceptable BMI would also be different.

Height

Although it may be usual for the taller man or woman to weigh more than a shorter person, this does not necessarily follow because bone structure, muscle girth and the percentage of bodyweight that is fat may all vary. In athletics, someone who is over six feet tall and slim is more likely to be a high jumper; someone of the same height who is a shot putter will be of a heavier build and weigh much more.

Bone structure

A person who has a small frame (small bone structure) is likely to weigh less than a person with a larger frame because bone is heavy. People have different bone structures and so cannot be expected to have similar weights.

Muscle girth

People naturally have different sized muscles (girth), measured around their widest point. A person with bigger muscles is likely to weigh more. So sports performers who require a lot of strength for their sport are likely to have larger muscles and therefore weigh more than others of similar height.

Weight related conditions

All the conditions below can be affected by diet and exercise.

Anorexia nervosa

Anorexia is an extreme condition. The person has a desire to lose body weight in a drive to become very slim or through loss of appetite. People who are anorexic can be in danger of losing muscle as well as fat.

Anorexics do not usually eat enough carbohydrate to provide the calories they need. If they do not get enough protein they will lose muscle and as a consequence their body shape (and somatotype) will change. Lack of vitamins and minerals (poor nutrition) can have important consequences. A lack of calcium, in particular, can affect the bones. Remember that health is not just 'the absence of disease and infirmity' but also 'a state of complete physical, social and mental wellbeing'. Anorexia is associated with psychological problems, so it can affect both the physical and mental health of the person.

Underweight

People who are underweight weigh less than is normal, healthy or required. Although some people may be underweight for their sport it is unlikely that they will be so severely underweight that they are defined as anorexic. Underweight in sport is more likely to be associated with jockeys and any sport which has weight categories, such as boxing.

Overweight

Overweight means being at a weight that is above normal for a person of that height and body type. Professional sports performers are often classed as overweight as a result of the additional muscle they have. This does not mean that they are overfat, however, as it is not their fat content that is high.

Overfat

Overfat is when a person weighs more than expected for a person of that height and too much of that weight is fat. This is a condition that gives concern.

Obese

Obese means a person who is very overfat. This is a condition which causes concern and is often in the news. People with this condition may find it difficult to exercise and take part in sport which makes losing weight even more difficult. Obesity is often brought about by not having a balanced lifestyle i.e. not having a good diet, and not being active enough. It can also be as a result of medical conditions.

People who are overweight regularly take part in sport at all levels. This may even be the reason they are overweight, for example they might have bigger and more developed muscles than other people. On the other hand, people who are overfat or obese may not be able to take part in sport. People who are overfat or obese would benefit from taking exercise because they could use up more calories than they take in.

Summary

It is important to know the definitions of each of the terms above relating to weight but also how they are related to optimum weight and to be able to explain them. As shown earlier a person's weight depends on their gender, bone structure and muscle. Wayne Rooney may well be considered to be overweight, but he is not overfat. Why? Because he has a large bone structure and greater muscle girth than other people of his height.

ResultsPlus
Exam tip

In terms of the examination questions, you should be able to give an example if required. Pick a sport that is easy to explain, such as horse racing or boxing. You might also be asked about the possible consequences of losing weight quickly to take part in competition. You should answer that this can cause dehydration, as jockeys/boxers may lose weight by sweating it out and so losing water content and not replacing it.

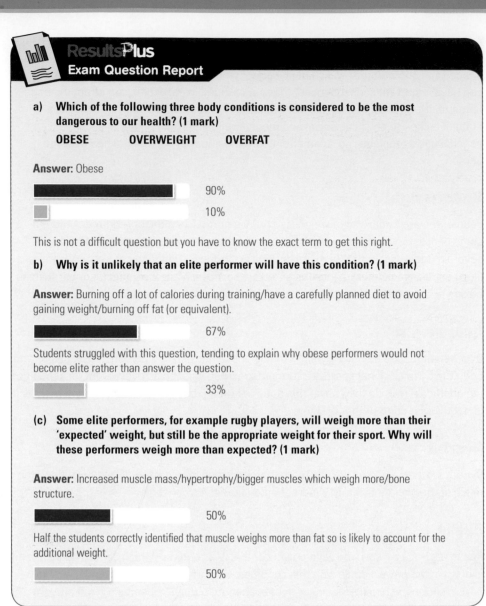

ResultsPlus
Exam Question Report

a) **Which of the following three body conditions is considered to be the most dangerous to our health? (1 mark)**

    OBESE   OVERWEIGHT   OVERFAT

Answer: Obese

████████████████	90%
██	10%

This is not a difficult question but you have to know the exact term to get this right.

b) **Why is it unlikely that an elite performer will have this condition? (1 mark)**

Answer: Burning off a lot of calories during training/have a carefully planned diet to avoid gaining weight/burning off fat (or equivalent).

██████████	67%

Students struggled with this question, tending to explain why obese performers would not become elite rather than answer the question.

█████	33%

(c) **Some elite performers, for example rugby players, will weigh more than their 'expected' weight, but still be the appropriate weight for their sport. Why will these performers weigh more than expected? (1 mark)**

Answer: Increased muscle mass/hypertrophy/bigger muscles which weigh more/bone structure.

███████	50%

Half the students correctly identified that muscle weighs more than fat so is likely to account for the additional weight.

███████	50%

Test yourself

4 a   Obese, overweight and overfat are all terms relating to body composition. Which of these three conditions is potentially the most harmful?

   b   Explain why an injured athlete's weight will increase if they maintain the same diet during injury as while training.

5 Obese is:

   A   having an excess of muscle which restricts mobility

   B   the percentage of body weight which is fat, muscle and bone

   C   muscles in a state of slight tension

   D   being very overfat

Performance enhancing and recreational drugs

 1.1.2d Explain the effects of smoking and alcohol on general health and on physical activity

 1.1.2e Know about different categories of drugs and the effects they may have on health, wellbeing and physical performance, and why some performers might risk using them

There are two types of drugs you need to know about:
1 performance-enhancing
2 recreational.

Performance-enhancing drugs

Drugs are taken to produce a particular effect. However, they may also have side effects – other effects that are not wanted and may be unpleasant.

The performance-enhancing drugs you need to know about are summarised in the following table.

Drug	Effect on performance	Sport	Side effects
Anabolic steroids	Able to train harder Recover quicker Build muscle faster than normal	Athletics	Increase chance of heart attack High blood pressure Infertility Liver damage
Beta blockers	Slow down heart rate Relaxing effect	Snooker Archery Shooting	Nausea and diarrhoea Tiredness Depression Low blood pressure
Diuretics	Lose weight through increased fluid loss	Boxing Horse racing	Dehydration Headaches Dizziness Kidney failure
Narcotics/ analgesics	Reduce pain, masking injury	Most sports	Loss of concentration, balance, coordination
Stimulants	Increase alertness Off-set lactic acid	American football	Insomnia Anxiety Irritability Increased and irregular heart rate High blood pressure
Peptide hormones (including erythropoietin)	Increase the number of red blood cells	Athletics Tour de France	Thicken the blood Increased risk of heart attack or stroke

edexcel ::: key terms

anabolic steroids Drugs that mimic the male sex hormone testosterone and promote bone and muscle growth.
beta blockers Drugs that are used to control heart rate and have a calming and relaxing effect.
diuretics Drugs that elevate the rate of urine excretion.
erythropoietin (EPO) A type of peptide hormone that increases the red blood cell count.
narcotic analgesics Drugs that can be used to reduce the feeling of pain.
peptide hormones Drugs that cause the production of other hormones.
stimulants Drugs that have an effect on the central nervous system, such as increased mental and/or physical alertness.

Why do sports persons take drugs?

Sports persons may decide to take drugs because:

1. drugs enhance their performance
2. drugs may help them to win and make a lot of money
3. they can perform at a higher level than without the aid of drugs.

Anabolic steroids

These drugs help to increase muscle mass and bone growth and allow the athlete to train harder. The result will be a fast and significant increase in muscular strength and power, vital in some sports. Steroids also allow the athlete to recover quicker and so train more often.

Anabolic steroids have side effects which include an increased chance of heart attack, high blood pressure, infertility and liver damage.

Beta blockers

Beta blockers slow the heart rate and so are associated with sports where steadiness is very important, such as archery, shooting and snooker.

Side effects include nausea and diarrhoea, tiredness, depression and low blood pressure.

Diuretics

Diuretics are used in sports where competitors must fit into weight categories. They can cause rapid weight loss by increasing the amount of urine produced. Diuretics are also sometimes taken to mask the presence of other banned drugs.

Side effects include dehydration, dizziness, muscle cramps, headaches and nausea. Long-term use can cause kidney damage.

Narcotics/analgesics

Narcotics, or analgesics, of which there are many, can help sports people return to training/competition more quickly by giving relief from pain after injury. They are banned because doing this may increase the risk of making the injury worse.

Side effects include loss of concentration, balance and coordination (motor skills), skills which sports persons cannot afford to lose if they are to compete at the highest levels.

Stimulants

In sport these may be taken to stimulate the central nervous system (CNS) thereby increasing alertness, and they can also be used to offset the effects of lactic acid on muscles.

Side effects include insomnia, irregular heartbeat, increased heart rate and high blood pressure.

Peptide hormones including erythropoietin (EPO)

These drugs, including erythropoietin or EPO, are used because they increase the number of red blood cells, which means they can carry more oxygen to working muscles. This is important in the longer distance events in athletics, for example.

A side effect of EPO is that it thickens the blood and can cause a heart attack or stroke.

Recreational drugs

The recreational drugs you need to know about are nicotine (smoking) and alcohol and their effects on general health and physical activity.

ResultsPlus

Exam tip

Many drugs are well-known as they are often in the news; testosterone and human growth hormone (HGH) are two. However, you will not be expected to name specific drugs in the examination.

Smoking

Smoking damages the whole cardiovascular system; the heart, the ability of the blood to carry oxygen, and the blood vessels. It increases blood pressure. It also damages the alveoli in the lungs and therefore the respiratory system. Smoking has been banned in public places since 2007 and the legal age for buying tobacco products is 18.

Side effects of smoking include cancer and coronary heart disease (CHD), a side effect which is both common and life threatening.

Alcohol

Alcohol can cause dehydration. Other short-term side effects are:

- calming effect
- produces extra urine
- impairs judgment
- reduces coordination
- reduces reaction time.

Alcohol has long-term effects on health, including cirrhosis of the liver which can result in death.

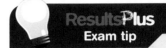

Results Plus
Exam tip

- Nicotine and alcohol are addictive and this is classed as a side effect.
- Alcohol is banned in some sports (e.g. shooting) as it can be used to give a calming effect. It is also banned in motor sports because it slows down reaction time.

Results Plus
Exam Question Report

1 (i) **Some athletes take illegal performance-enhancing drugs to control heart rate. Which class of drug will have a calming effect on a performer's heart rate? (1 mark)**

Answer: Beta blockers

████████████	79%

Students who got this wrong tended to give 'steroids' or 'narcotic analgesics' as their answer. Few were aware of the effects of beta blockers.

████	21%

(ii) **A potentially harmful effect of another class of drug is to increase heart rate. Name this class of drug. (1 mark)**

Answer: Stimulants

████████████	77%

The majority of students got this wrong. You need to know the side effects of each drug as well as the desired effect: a side effect of taking a stimulant is **an increased or irregular heart rate**.

████	23%

Test yourself

6 Give three side effects of smoking on the cardiovascular system.

7 Give one side effect of smoking on the respiratory system.

8 Excessive use of alcohol can damage the liver. Which of the following is the condition caused to the liver in this way?

Lordosis   Kyphosis   Cirrhosis   Scoliosis

9 A stimulant is a category of drug.

a Why might an athlete take a stimulant?
b Give one side effect of taking a stimulant.

10 Injury is often a problem for athletes. Some drugs can help them recover more quickly. What type of drug are these?

Risk assessment and preventing injuries

 1.2.1f **Identify risks associated with participation in physical activities, and explain how to reduce these risks to maintain wellbeing**

Warm-up and cool-down

- You may be asked a question about warming up in this section of the examination as it is one of the ways to prevent injury.

- Cooling down does not prevent injury but does help to disperse lactic acid after exercise and prevent muscle soreness.

Equipment and facilities

If you are playing in an organised event it is the responsibility of the officials to make sure the equipment and facilities are safe. If you are taking part in an individual activity, you should check that it is safe before you start. These checks vary depending on the activity.

- **Equipment**: in cricket, officials need to check that the ball has not been tampered with. In gymnastics, equipment must be stable and secure. In football, the referee would check the players' studs.

- **Facilities**: in football, rugby and hockey, the playing surface must not be frozen or dangerous.

Protective equipment and clothing

The first and most obvious method of injury prevention in most activities is to wear the protective equipment suitable for that sport; if you play cricket, this would be a good choice to give as an example. In some sports protective clothing or equipment is compulsory. Examples include shin pads in football and a batting or wicket keeper's helmet in cricket.

Wearing the correct clothing means having the most suitable clothing for a sport, which should minimise the risks. For example, wearing the right footwear for the surface you are performing on could prevent you from slipping. In road running, the right shoes give you adequate support.

In terms of risk assessment it is important to know the obvious. For example, wearing a wristwatch or jewellery could be dangerous both to the person wearing it, a partner or team mate, and an opponent. Other obvious but all too often neglected items that come into this category include footwear. Running shoes can be expensive but modern technology has made it possible to produce training and running shoes that protect the feet and joints much more than used to be the case. A track suit is essential when warming up in cold weather to help prevent pulled muscles before and to prevent getting cold after the activity or competition.

Balancing competition

Competition is balanced to make it fair and safe.

Before a competition the organisers are obliged to take into account the risks and safety requirements necessary; this may be as simple as balancing the competition regarding ability or grade, in combat sports for example. In a league competition this is taken into account almost automatically with promotion of the strongest teams and relegation of the weaker ones.

Weight

In some sports competitors are matched by weight. Boxing is the obvious example, but other combat sports also use weight categories.

Gender

Most sports that involve physical contact, including football and rugby, are played in single sex groups, as are most racket games. This is to ensure safety as the different weights, sizes and physiques of men and women could lead to injuries during contact. However, tennis, badminton and table tennis offer mixed competition, as does hockey.

Age

In school sport, age is one of the main factors in balancing competition. As the growth spurt comes early for some students it often results in quite unequal competition. In women's gymnastics, the competitors have to be 16 years old during the year of competition as being small is seen to be an advantage in this sport.

Handicap

Golf is unique in that the handicap system that measures ability means that players of different ability levels, age and gender could in effect play against each other and have a fair outcome.

Playing to the rules of the competition

Why have rules? Rules in games have been devised so that competition will be safe and fair. Remember that the officials are there to make sure this takes place.

PAR-Q

The Physical Activity Readiness Questionnaire (PAR-Q) is a way of making sure people are ready to start exercising safely by assessing their current level of health and fitness.

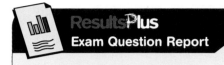

ResultsPlus
Exam Question Report

Competitions are often balanced.
(i) Explain the term balanced competition. (1 mark)

Answer: (i) Trying to make sure that opposing players/teams are evenly matched.

49%

Marks were mainly lost through lack of explanation; for instance, giving an example of age or weight rather than an explanation. You will not get a mark if you put 'balancing sides' as this does not explain the term 'balanced'.

51%

(ii) State three ways that competition can be balanced. (3 marks)

Answer: (ii) By skill/ability levels, weight, age or gender.

22%
0–1 marks

No more than one correct way was given. There was some minor confusion over weight and height categories. There are no competitions balanced by competitor height.

23%
2 marks

Two out of three correct ways given.

55%
3 marks

Over half of students correctly gave three ways of balancing competition.

Test yourself

11 Referees and umpires help prevent injury to players by enforcing the rules of an activity.

a The chances of becoming injured are also reduced by balancing competition. Explain the term 'balancing competition'.

b State **four** ways that competition in activities could be balanced.

c Name an activity of your choice, giving specific examples of **two** ways in which competition within the activity is balanced.

d State **three** other ways, apart from playing to the rules and balancing competition, in which performers can reduce the risk of injury.

1.2.2: A healthy, active lifestyle and your cardiovascular system

Need more help?
For more on this topic, see pages 114–127.

✓ 1.2.2a **Understand the immediate and short-term effects of exercise and physical activity on the cardiovascular system**

✓ 1.2.2b **Understand the long-term effects of exercise and physical activity on the cardiovascular system**

The cardiovascular system

The heart is a muscular pump that pumps blood away from the heart around the body through a system of arteries which take oxygen rich blood and nutrients to the muscles to allow them to work.

The blood then picks up carbon dioxide (a waste product) from the muscles and carries this back to the heart in veins. From there it is pumped to the lungs where it is breathed out and in exchange oxygen is breathed in. This process is called gaseous exchange; you will revise it in Topic 1.2.3 (pages 59–61).

This process takes place because muscles need energy in the form of oxygen and nutrients to produce movement. Carbon dioxide and other waste products are produced when we exercise. The cardiovascular system enables us to get rid of the waste products and supplies the muscles with the oxygen and nutrients they need to continue to work.

Immediate and short term effects of participation in exercise and physical activity on the cardiovascular system

During exercise muscles need more oxygen, therefore the heart needs to beat more strongly and quickly.

Our heart rate is raised by the release of the hormone adrenaline. Adrenaline is the reason why the heart can beat faster in stressful situations. The rise in heart rate enables more blood to be pumped quickly around the body and to the lungs, so that more oxygen and nutrients can be circulated and waste products removed. Training helps the body to cope better in these situations, as the heart of a fit person will be bigger, stronger and more used to working under such stress.

Blood pressure

The heart beats more strongly during exercise, causing blood pressure to rise and become higher.

Blood pressure has two parts, systolic and diastolic.

- Systolic is the high pressure measured when the blood is pumped out of the heart to go around the body. This high number rises during exercise and falls during sleep.

- Diastolic pressure is when the heart relaxes between beats, so this is the low number on a reading.

edexcel ⠿ key terms

blood pressure The force exerted by circulating blood on the walls of the blood vessels.
cardiac output The amount of blood ejected from the heart in one minute.
heart rate (pulse rate) The number of times the heart beats per minute.
stroke volume The volume of blood pumped out of the heart by each ventricle during one contraction.

ResultsPlus
Watch out!

Remember that heart rate is the number of times the heart beats per minute, not the number of times the heart beats. Students lose marks for forgetting to add the words 'per minute'.

Regular exercise and the cardiovascular system

Regular exercise enables the cardiovascular system to become stronger and more efficient as it adapts to the increased demands of the body. The changes that take place are listed below.

1 Stroke volume (the amount of blood pumped by the heart with each beat) increases.

2 Cardiac output (the amount of blood pumped by the heart each minute) increases.

These two terms and heart rate are related by the following formula which you **must know and be able to explain**:

Heart rate × stroke volume = cardiac output (or HR × SV = CO)

The number of times your heart beats per minute x the amount the heart pumps with each beat = the amount of blood your heart pumps each minute

3 Resting heart rate decreases. Resting heart rate is lower in people who train regularly because their hearts can pump more blood with each beat.

4 Size of heart increases. Exercising and training causes the heart to adapt and become larger and stronger.

5 Cardiac output increases as a result of regular training. This is another benefit of regular exercise and physical activity on the cardiovascular system.

6 Time taken for heart rate to return to normal after exercise decreases. As the heart is bigger and stronger (increased stroke volume and cardiac output) it can also recover more quickly after a training session.

7 Blood pressure is reduced. Although blood pressure rises during exercise, regular exercise helps to strengthen the heart by pumping more blood per beat (stroke volume), so the heart does not have to work so hard and the stress on the arteries is less, therefore lowering normal resting blood pressure. Regular exercise may also lead to weight loss which can also help to lower blood pressure.

8 Veins and arteries are healthy. One of the ways in which exercise reduces the risk of coronary heart disease is by helping the blood vessels to become more flexible and efficient.

ResultsPlus
Exam Question Report

1. **During exercise Katie's cardiac output increases, compared with when she is at rest.**
   (i) What is meant by the term cardiac output? (1 mark)

Answer: The amount of blood ejected from the heart in one minute/HR x SV/Heart Rate multiplied by Stroke Volume.

| | 68% |

Many students answered 'The amount of blood pumped around the body in one minute' which is incorrect; answers should refer to the heart specifically. Those that did not understand the term 'cardiac output' could not accurately answer part (ii).

| | 11% |

Only a limited number of candidates gave the correct explanation.

Test yourself

1 a Define the term 'heart rate'.

  b What will happen to an individual's heart rate at the start of a training session?

  c What effect will this have on cardiac output?

  d Explain why it is important for an individual that the heart rate alters in this way.

2 What long-term effect would regular training have on **resting** heart rate and stroke volume?

The effects of lifestyle on the cardiovascular system

✓ **1.2.2c** Understand the impact of rest on the cardiovascular system

✓ **1.2.2d** Understand the impact of diet on the cardiovascular system

✓ **1.2.2e** Understand the impact of recreational drugs on the cardiovascular system

edexcel ▦ **key terms**

rest The period of time allocated to recovery.

Rest

You have seen that rest (the time you allow for recovery to take place) and recovery are two principles of training that work together to allow the body to adapt to exercise and training. The same applies to the cardiovascular system. Rest allows the heart to increase in size and the number of capillaries to increase.

Diet – cholesterol

In Topic 1.1.5 you learned about the factors of a balanced diet and that it is important to avoid too much unsaturated fat and animal fat as these foods are high in cholesterol. High cholesterol levels may increase the risk of coronary heart disease.

Cholesterol is a fatty substance carried in the blood by lipoproteins. Lipoproteins come in two forms:

HDL (high density lipoprotein)

LDL (low density lipoprotein).

Not all cholesterol is bad. HDL is known as the 'good' cholesterol because it takes cholesterol away from the blood vessels. LDL, or 'bad' cholesterol, builds up in the arteries, making them less flexible and making it more difficult for the blood to pass through. If a clot eventually forms then the blood cannot pass through and a heart attack or a stroke can occur.

There is a link between cholesterol and high blood pressure as a combination of the two can lead to a heart attack or a stroke.

ResultsPlus
Exam tip

You need to know that:
HDL is the good cholesterol and why it is good.
LDL is the bad cholesterol and why it is bad.

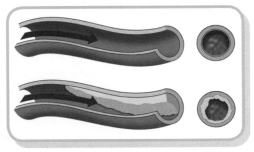

Cholesterol builds up in the artery.

Recreational drugs

Nicotine is the drug found in tobacco. Smoking a cigarette increases heart rate and blood pressure; high blood pressure is just one of the long-term effects of smoking. Nicotine also reduces the amount of HDL, the good cholesterol, in the blood, so smoking combined with a diet high in LDL can seriously increase the possibility of heart disease.

Alcohol can also have a variety of adverse affects on health. Drinking too much on a regular basis could affect cardiovascular health by causing an increase in blood pressure.

ResultsPlus
Exam tip

You should be able to relate this back to other topics, especially topic 1.1.1 'Healthy, active lifestyles and how they could benefit you'. This section links very much to the reasons for and benefits of exercise. Cardiovascular training is connected with production of the 'feel good' hormone serotonin, and so is a mental as well as a physical benefit. It is also closely linked to health, 'a state of complete physical, social and mental wellbeing, not merely the absence of disease and infirmity'.

Test yourself

3   What adaptation occurs to the heart from rest?

4   Which type of cholesterol is described as 'good'?

1.2.3: A healthy, active lifestyle and your respiratory system

1.2.3a **Understand the immediate and short-term effects on the respiratory system of participation in exercise and physical activity**

1.2.3b **Understand the long-term effects of regular exercise and physical activity on the respiratory system**

1.2.3c **Understand the impact of recreational drugs on the respiratory system**

The respiratory system

The respiratory system works with the cardiovascular system and is very important in relation to health, fitness and performance.

When we breathe in, the muscles between our ribs contract causing our chest to expand upwards and outwards. At the same time the diaphragm contracts; it flattens and lowers, changing from a dome to a flat shape. When the ribs lift upwards and outwards the lungs are pulled outwards also. As the pressure inside the lungs is reduced, air rushes in through the nose and mouth.

As the air passes through the nose it is filtered by the hairs, warmed by the blood vessels and moistened by water vapour before passing through a tube called the trachea. The trachea branches left and right into the bronchi which take air to the left and right lung. The trachea and the bronchi also contain microscopic hairs, which are covered with mucus to ensure that the air is cleaned. The bronchi branch off into smaller and smaller bronchioles until at the very end they reach the tiny sacs called alveoli.

Alveoli

The lining of the alveoli is very thin and must be moist and clean in order to work efficiently. If this is not the case, the exchange of gases (oxygen and carbon dioxide) will not work effectively, which will affect our performance in activities and games. It will also affect our general health. For example, people with respiratory conditions may become breathless easily.

The respiratory system

Oxygen gets into the blood stream via the capillaries around the alveoli.

Once it is in the blood it can get to the muscles where it is needed.

alveoli   capillaries   ribs

Gaseous exchange

The air we breathe in is rich in oxygen, which is delivered to the alveoli in the lungs. The alveoli are surrounded by capillaries (very narrow tubes) that carry blood. Oxygen in the alveoli diffuses into the deoxygenated blood. Haemoglobin then carries oxygen around the body. At the same time, carbon dioxide diffuses out of the blood into the alveoli. This carbon dioxide is then breathed out in exhaled air. This process is called gaseous exchange.

Need more help?
For more on this topic, see pages 128–135.

edexcel ::: **key terms**

EPO (erythropoietin) A type of peptide hormone that increases the red blood cell count.
Oxygen debt The amount of oxygen consumed during recovery above that which would have ordinarily been consumed in the same time at rest (this results in a shortfall in the oxygen available).

Results**Plus**
Exam tip

It is important to know how this process will help sports people. Fitter people will cope better with gaseous exchange, getting more oxygen in and more carbon dioxide out per breath. EPO helps to produce more red blood cells so it helps to attract more oxygen during gaseous exchange, but it is an illegal drug in sports.

Immediate and short term effects of participation in exercise and physical activity

When taking part in exercise or strenuous activity the body immediately reacts. The respiratory system responds in two main ways.

Breathing becomes faster, deeper and stronger

We breathe more frequently and more deeply when exercising hard. An increased breathing rate helps get more oxygen to the working muscles. However, if you work hard enough for long enough you will reach a point where you cannot get enough oxygen and your muscles will stop working. An example of this is when you get cramp and have to stop.

Oxygen debt

Intense exercise requires more glucose and oxygen, and more waste is produced. Your heart beats faster, and you breathe more deeply, in an attempt to provide more oxygen and nutrients to the working muscles.

If the muscles cannot get enough oxygen through breathing, the body finds energy using a different method, called anaerobic respiration. This leads to the build up of lactic acid and produces an 'oxygen debt' that needs to be repaid.

Oxygen debt is the amount of oxygen consumed during recovery above that which would normally have been used at rest. If the lactic acid cannot be dispersed, the muscles will ache and eventually cramp will occur and the performer will have to stop.

To repay the oxygen debt built up, you will breathe deeper and quicker, to take in more oxygen. You will need to rest until the blood can bring sufficient oxygen to the muscles, and your performance may be affected.

> To summarise: lactic acid builds up; muscles begin to ache; oxygen debt occurs, leading to cramp.

Effects of regular participation and long term benefits of participation

Regular training results in a more efficient respiratory system, which can cope with the effects of exercise more easily. It also brings about other adaptations:

- it improves the efficiency of the lungs and increases lung capacity

- it increases tidal volume – the amount of air breathed in and out of the lungs with each breath

- it increases vital capacity – the largest amount of air that can be breathed in and out of the lungs by the most forceful inspiration and expiration

- it increases the number of alveoli available for gaseous exchange so more oxygen is available for the working muscles and the process becomes more efficient.

The effects of smoking on the respiratory system

Smoking can damage the lungs, especially the alveoli, which become less stretchy so they cannot take in as much oxygen or get rid of carbon dioxide as easily. This means the process of gaseous exchange is less efficient. The person becomes short of breath and their heart has to pump harder to get the oxygen their body needs.

ResultsPlus
Exam Question Report

1 (d) Which of the following statements correctly identifies the effects of smoking on sports performers?

A Carbon dioxide in cigarette smoke reduces oxygen available to the muscles.
B Haemoglobin prefers carbon monoxide so more oxygen is carried out of the lungs.
C Cardiovascular endurance is not affected by smoking, but speed is, so the sprinter cannot run as fast.
D Recovery in endurance athletes is slower as a reduced amount of oxygen gets to the muscles due to carbon monoxide in cigarette smoke.

Answer: D

　65%

Smoking reduces the amount of oxygen taken in, therefore it takes the athlete longer to recover from exercise.

　35%

Many students could not identify the effects of smoking on the respiratory system.

Test yourself

1 a During a match a player is likely to build up an oxygen debt. What is oxygen debt?
　b If a player has built up an oxygen debt will they have been working aerobically or anaerobically?
　c What by-product is associated with oxygen debt?
　d State two ways the performer could help to remove this by-product.

1.2.4: A healthy, active lifestyle and your muscular system

1.2.4a **Understand the role of the muscular system during physical activity and how major muscle groups benefit from particular types of activity**

1.2.4b **Understand the role of muscles in movement**

The muscular system

Muscles are the driving force behind movement. You need to remember 11 muscles for the examination – the same number as players in a football team.

The 11 muscles you need to know are called voluntary (or skeletal) muscles because we can control them (skeletal because they are attached to the skeleton). Involuntary muscles, for example those in the gut, are involved with processes we cannot control, such as digestion. Cardiac muscle is found only in the heart and is concerned with the circulatory system.

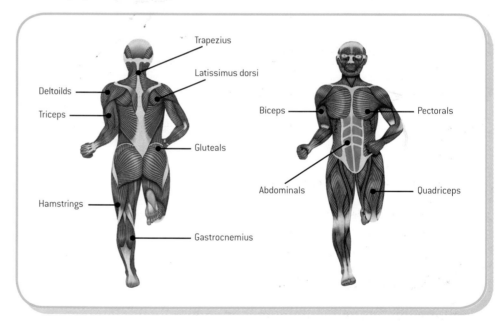

Muscles are attached to bones by tendons. They must contract for movement to take place. When they contract and pull, the muscle shortens and thickens. Try it: with your arm straight, contract your bicep muscle. The result should be that your elbow flexes (bends) and your bicep shortens and thickens. To straighten your arm again you need to contract your tricep, which will pull your arm straight (extension).

To allow movement both ways, the bicep and tricep work together as an **antagonistic pair**; i.e. when one muscle contracts the other relaxes. The hamstring and quadricep are also arranged as an antagonistic pair.

Need more help?
For more on this topic, see pages 136–149.

edexcel ⠿ key terms

isometric contraction When the muscle contracts but stays in a fixed position.
isotonic contraction Muscle contraction that results in limb movement.

ResultsPlus
Watch out!

Remember muscles can pull but they cannot push.

When you contract your bicep, your arm flexes at the elbow, and so movement takes place. This is called an **isotonic contraction**.

If muscles contract and no movement takes place this is called an **isometric contraction**. Demonstrate this to yourself: with your elbow flexed at 90 degrees, contract your bicep but keep the same angle at the elbow. The result this time will be that, as you contract your bicep, the muscle shortens and thickens but no movement occurs. This is known as an **isometric contraction**.

Results Plus
Exam tip

To help you remember the muscles in the body, break them down into smaller sections, such as 1:4:2:4. Recall them starting from the top of your body and finishing in the lower leg.

Results Plus
Exam Question Report

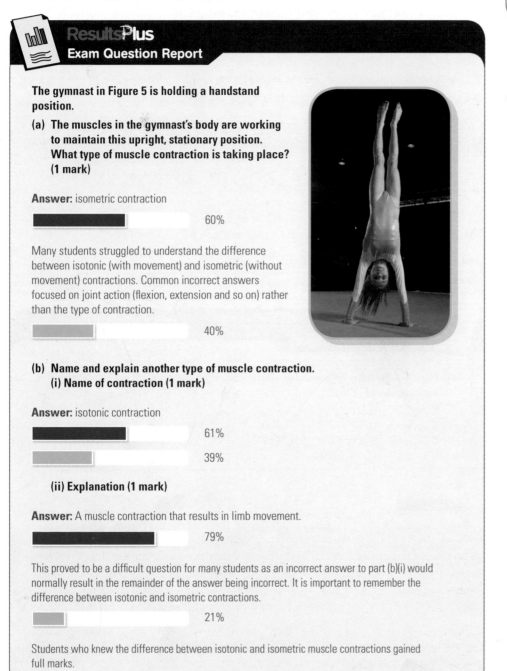

The gymnast in Figure 5 is holding a handstand position.

(a) **The muscles in the gymnast's body are working to maintain this upright, stationary position. What type of muscle contraction is taking place? (1 mark)**

Answer: isometric contraction

60%

Many students struggled to understand the difference between isotonic (with movement) and isometric (without movement) contractions. Common incorrect answers focused on joint action (flexion, extension and so on) rather than the type of contraction.

40%

(b) **Name and explain another type of muscle contraction.**
   (i) Name of contraction (1 mark)

Answer: isotonic contraction

61%

39%

   (ii) Explanation (1 mark)

Answer: A muscle contraction that results in limb movement.

79%

This proved to be a difficult question for many students as an incorrect answer to part (b)(i) would normally result in the remainder of the answer being incorrect. It is important to remember the difference between isotonic and isometric contractions.

21%

Students who knew the difference between isotonic and isometric muscle contractions gained full marks.

The 11 muscles you need to know about each bring about an individual movement when they contract and pull on a bone. The movement produced could be abduction, adduction, flexion, rotation or extension (see 1.2.5, pages 68–70).

Muscle	Action produced	A sporting example
1) Deltoid	Abducts (takes away) the upper arm from the body	Serving in tennis when the arm goes above the head
2) Trapezius	Rotates the shoulder blades (and scapular) backwards	Rowing
3) Latissimus dorsi	Rotates upper arm at the shoulders	Swimming butterfly
4) Pectoral muscle	Adducts the arm	Swimming front crawl
5) Abdominal muscles	Flexes and rotates trunk	Rowing
6) Biceps	Flexes arm at the elbow	Bending the arm to throw a cricket ball
7) Triceps	Extends arm at the elbow	Straightening the arm to throw a cricket ball
8) Gluteus maximus	Extends the upper leg	Running
9) Quadriceps	Extends the leg at the knee	Kicking a football
10) Hamstrings	Flexes the leg at the knee	Sprinting
11) Gastrocnemius	Plantar flexes the foot	Running – pushing onto the toes

ResultsPlus
Exam tip

If you are not sure what movement a muscle makes, be prepared to do the actions in the examination.

ResultsPlus
Exam Question Report

1 (j) Which of the following muscles allows abduction of the arm at the shoulder during a tennis serve?

A Latissimus dorsi
B Pectorals
C Deltoids
D Triceps

Answer: C

42%

Students normally do very well on multiple-choice questions but a lot of students found this one difficult. It is essential to understand what movement each muscle brings about, and to what limb.

The effects of exercise on the muscular system

✓ 1.2.4c **Understand the immediate and short-term effects on the muscular system of participation in exercise and physical activity**

✓ 1.2.4d **Understand the long-term effects of regular exercise and physical activity on the muscular system**

✓ 1.2.4e **Understand the potential for muscle injuries through exercise and physical activity and know common techniques for treatment**

✓ 1.2.4f **Understand the impacts of rest, diet and performance-enhancing drugs on the muscular system**

Immediate effects of exercise

- During exercise muscles contract isometrically and isotonically.
- As a result the muscles need more fuel – oxygen and energy.
- If muscles cannot get enough oxygen, lactic acid is produced and muscles go into oxygen debt.
- When lactic acid builds up it can lead to muscle stiffness and soreness.

The effects of regular training on the muscular system

Muscles will adapt and get bigger through exercise and training, such as lifting free weights. This process is called muscle hypertrophy. It results in the muscle becoming stronger (muscular strength) and able to work for longer without getting tired (muscular endurance).

Injuries to the muscular system

Injury to a muscle – such as tearing the muscle fibres – is called a 'soft tissue' injury. The most common type is a muscle strain, which usually occurs if a muscle is stretched further than normal or worked hard without a proper warm-up.

Injury to a muscle can result in loss of fitness and **muscle atrophy** (loss of muscle size and strength). This is an example of the principle of reversibility (see page 127). Muscle atrophy also occurs slowly if the intensity or frequency of training is reduced. Increased training will cause muscle hypertrophy, meaning an increase in the size of the muscle.

You need to know how to prevent these injuries and what to do if they do occur.

Prevention

Warming up the muscles slowly by stretching them helps to prevent injury in the main activity (the next part of the exercise session). Cooling down gradually at the end of the training session or performance disperses any build-up of lactic acid, avoiding muscle stiffness either later or the next day.

Treatment

The RICE treatment for muscle injuries will be revised in the next topic.

edexcel ▦ **key terms**

anabolic steroids Drugs that mimic the male sex hormone testosterone and promote bone and muscle growth.

 Results**Plus**
Exam tip

Building muscular strength means lifting heavy weights with few repetitions and building muscular endurance means lifting lighter weights with more repetitions.

Results**Plus**
Watch out!

Remember you strain a muscle and sprain a joint (such as your ankle).

Lifestyle, performance-enhancing drugs and the muscular system

The principles of rest and recovery are as important as exercise and training when building muscles. Exercise causes damage. If muscles are to repair and build (and get bigger and stronger), they need time to recover and for adaptations to occur.

Diet

Protein in the diet also aids recovery. Protein helps muscles rebuild and repair after exercise, as well as building muscle. It is therefore very important for anyone who needs to build and maintain muscle.

Performance-enhancing drugs

Performance-enhancing drugs build muscle strength and power. In body building they are used to increase muscle size (hypertrophy). Increased power and strength help athletes in events such as sprinting and throwing and some performers take **anabolic steroids** – which are of course illegal – for this reason. These drugs also enable a quicker recovery.

Test yourself

1 Which of the following terms is correct to describe muscles getting bigger?

A Atrophy

B Fast twitch

C Slow twitch

D Hypertrophy

2 Figure 1 shows a performer completing a press up, as part of a circuit training programme.

Position A shows the performer lowering his body to the ground.
Position B shows the performer supporting his body weight in a stationary position.

What type of muscle contraction is taking place in the arms as the performer:

a lowers his weight to Position A?

b supports his weight in Position B?

3 When sprinting, an athlete's muscles work antagonistically. Complete the following statements to explain what is happening when the athlete is sprinting.

a When muscles work antagonistically, one muscle _____ and the other muscle _____ .

b As the muscles work they change the shape of the leg at the knee. When the leg straightens it is called _____ and when it bends it is called _____ .

c The muscles responsible for straightening the leg at the knee are the _____ . The _____ bend the leg at the knee.

1.2.5: A healthy, active lifestyle and your skeletal system

✓ **1.2.5a** Understand the function of the skeletal system for movement, support or protection during physical activity

✓ **1.2.5b** Understand the ranges of movement at joints during physical activity

The functions of the skeleton

The skeleton gives shape to the body and is part of our body composition ('the percentage of our body that is fat muscle and **bone**'). The skeletal system includes all the bones in the body and has three main functions.

1 **Movement**
   Bones allow movement to take place and muscles help to bring this movement about.

   Bones are joined to other bones by ligaments, which give the joints stability and allow movement. Bones that are joined together in this way and are involved in movement are called long bones. Muscles are attached to these bones by tendons. Muscles pulling on bones cause us to move.

2 **Support**
   The skeleton supports the body in different positions – sitting, standing, walking, running and various combinations of these. The skeletal system gives the body shape.

3 **Protection**
   An important function of the skeleton is protection. When taking part in sport we often put our bodies in some danger but our skeleton helps to protect us. If we get hit in the chest by a ball when playing a game, our heart and lungs are protected by our rib cage. Our skull (cranium) protects our brain, from a clash of heads in football for example.

Joints and joint movement

How joints work

The definition of a joint is a place where two or more bones meet. Movement around a joint is caused by muscles pulling on the bones that make up the joint. Joints have cartilage at the ends to protect them and avoid friction (stop them rubbing together). They are lubricated by a substance called synovial fluid.

Types of joints

You need to know about two types of joint:
* hinge
* ball and socket.

Specifically, you should understand how the hinge joints at the elbow and knee and the ball and socket joint at the shoulder work. *The hip joint is also a ball and socket joint but it is best if you use the shoulder to answer questions as this is what is specifically required.*

Need more help?
For more on this topic, see pages 150–165.

edexcel ⸬ key terms

joint A place where two or more bones meet.

Results**Plus**
Exam tip

For the examination you should be able to explain movement, support and protection. You also need to know how to apply them to an example. You may be asked a question where you can choose your own sport as an example, or you may be told which sport to use. In these questions take the information you have learned and apply it logically.

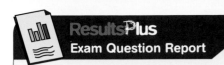

One function of the skeleton is to allow movement. Complete the table below by:
(i)   naming two other functions of the skeleton
(ii) explaining how the functions are achieved
(iii) describing the importance of the function to a badminton player.

(i) Function of skeleton	(ii) Explanation of how function is achieved	(iii) Importance in badminton
Movement	Muscle attachment to bones	Hitting action when playing a shot needs movement
Protection	Bones protect the vital organs	If struck or they fall and hit their head (the brain is protected by the skull)
Support	Provides rigid framework to hold body upright	Allows the player to hold body upright while reaching for shuttle

(5 marks)
Answers: See above table.

▮▮▮▮   25%   Level 1, 0–1

Some candidates did not read the question thoroughly and used other sports such as football to explain the importance of the skeleton. Others gave very vague answers to part (iii) that were not applied to the context of the question; for example, that the bones protected from injury if they fell.

▮▮▮▮▮▮   42%   Level 2, 2–3

Most candidates gained at least two marks for this question by recognising the role of the skeleton in terms of protection, and explaining that it protects the vital organs.

▮▮▮▮   33%   Level 3, 4–5

A good answer should give two clear functions, with a clear explanation of how they are achieved and relating this specifically to badminton.

Movement possibilities

Each joint has movement potential. These movements have specific names:

* flexion

* extension

* abduction

* adduction

* rotation.

You must know which movements are possible at the three joints and be able to apply them to actions in physical activity. For example, the joint action at the shoulder of a cricketer when bowling the ball is rotation. You may not know about cricket but you must be able to work this out. There will probably be a photograph to help you.

Joint actions

You must know the actions possible at the three joints mentioned above: shoulder, elbow and knee. You should be able to work them out from the following information.

Joint action and explanation	Description of movement	Sporting example
Flexion – the angle at the joint gets smaller	If your elbow or the knee is straight and then bent the action is flexion	Bending the knees before jumping in basketball
Extension – the angle at the joint gets bigger	If your elbow or knee is bent and then straightened the action is extension	Straightening the leg when kicking a ball in football
Abduction – means moving a limb away from the body	If your arms are straight and by your sides and then you take them out sideways **away** from your body that is abduction	In circuit training, doing astride jumps over and onto a bench - abduction is when you have your legs and arms wide.
Adduction – means bringing a limb towards the body	If both your arms are straight and sideways away from your body and then you bring them **towards** your body that is adduction.	In circuit training, doing astride jumps over and onto a bench - adduction is when you have your arms by your sides and your legs together on the bench.
Rotation – means moving in a circular action	If you swing your arms round in a forwards or backwards direction the action is rotation	Bowling in cricket

Joint	shoulder	elbow	knee
flexion	yes	yes	yes
extension	yes	yes	yes
abduction	yes	no	no
adduction	yes	no	no
rotation	yes	no	no

What joint actions are taking place when the tennis player hits the ball?

Look at the photo above. Consider what joint actions are taking place when the shot is played. As the left arm goes back (abduction), the right arm goes towards the body (adduction). As the shot is played, the movement is reversed. There is flexion then extension at the elbow as it bends then straightens. There is also flexion and extension at the knees. When she serves, there is rotation at the shoulders.

Exercise and the skeletal system

✓ 1.2.5c **Understand the effects of regular exercise and physical activity on the skeletal system**

✓ 1.2.5d **Understand the importance of weight-bearing exercise to prevent osteoporosis**

✓ 1.2.5e **Understand the potential for skeletal injuries through exercise and physical activity and know common techniques for treatment**

✓ 1.2.5f **Understand the impact of diet on the skeletal system**

Exercise is important for all the systems of the body, including the skeletal system.

- Exercise helps to increase bone density, making bones stronger and more able to withstand greater forces or more frequent training.

- Exercise strengthens ligaments (which join bone to bone) and tendons (which join muscles to bone). Injuries to ligaments and tendons cause incapacity and often take a long time to repair.

It is important to use exercises that benefit the skeletal system. Sitting down exercises such as cycling or supported exercise such as swimming are excellent for the cardiovascular and respiratory systems but less beneficial for the skeletal system. Exercises that require us to bear our own body weight, such as aerobics, yoga, pilates, running, skipping or walking are more beneficial to the skeletal system.

Osteoporosis and the importance of weight-bearing exercises

Osteoporosis is a debilitating condition of the bones, which can result in them breaking more easily. It is mostly associated with older people because over time bones become lighter and their strength is reduced. Suitable weight-bearing exercise, including the activities mentioned above and others such as weight training, can help to prevent osteoporosis, and also prevent it from getting worse.

The definition of flexibility is 'the range of movement possible at a joint' and this is another important part of exercise for the skeletal system. Individuals become stiff in their joints if they do not exercise. Stretching is the obvious way to do this, but activities such as yoga and pilates are excellent and have the added advantage of improving strength and balance.

Injuries to the skeletal system and the importance of diet

There are two types of injury to the skeletal system: **fractures** and **joint injuries**.

Fractures

There are four types of fractures: compound, greenstick, simple and stress.

A **fracture** is: a broken or cracked bone		Cause: usually a blow or severe twisting	
Symptoms	Pain, inability to move, tenderness, swelling, sometimes deformity		
Types	Compound	Greenstick	Simple	Stress
	Broken bone comes through the skin	Break only part way across the bone	Fracture in one line, no displacement	Overuse injuries usually in weight bearing areas, such as the lower leg – shin

edexcel ::: key terms

RICE Rest, Ice, Compression, Elevation (a method of treating injuries)

Results Plus
Watch out!

Remember: Tendons join muscle to bone. Ligaments join bone to bone.

Joint injuries

There are five types of joint injuries: tennis elbow, golfer's elbow, dislocation, sprain and torn cartilage. Although they are not all related to bones, they are all related to the skeletal system, which includes tendons and ligaments.

Tennis and golfer's elbow

Both are injuries to the tendons at the elbow joint (remember tendons join muscle to bone) and involve overuse. The symptoms for golfer's elbow are pain on the *inside* of the elbow. The symptoms for tennis elbow are pain on the *outside* of the elbow. Rest is important in the treatment of these injuries.

Dislocation

The bone at a joint comes out of place, usually as the result of a hard blow. The first obvious sign/symptom is deformity and swelling; there is a lot of pain around the injury.

Sprains

A sprain is damage to the ligament at a joint (remember ligaments join bone to bone). A sprained ankle is quite a common example of this injury. These injuries can occur from a blow but also from twisting, for example at the ankle, knee or wrist.

Symptoms include swelling and pain around the joint.

Torn cartilage

Cartilage is found at the end of the bones and helps to avoid friction. Sometimes it tears (most commonly on the inside of the knee), for example if a player spins quickly. It is a very painful injury, and often results in swelling.

Treatment for joint injuries

The RICE treatment can be used to treat minor joint injuries and prevent them getting worse.

The letters of RICE stand for:

Rest – stop playing or exercising. Playing on with an injury is probably the worst thing to do so that is why rest is the first thing to do.

Ice – one of the symptoms mentioned for many of the injuries is swelling and another is pain, putting ice on the injured part will help to stop these to some extent. Ice, a bag of frozen peas or a cold spray are suitable for this.

Compression – putting pressure on the ice pack also helps to reduce the swelling and the pain.

Elevation – raising the injured part will also contribute to keeping the swelling down.

Diet and the skeletal system

The skeletal system needs calcium and vitamin D. Calcium is a mineral and is essential to a balanced diet. It helps to build strong bones, increase bone density and ward off osteoporosis. Vitamin D helps to maintain healthy bones and helps calcium to be absorbed.

Calcium is found in milk, cheese and yoghurt. Vitamin D is made by the body when the skin is exposed to sunlight, hence it is known as the sunshine vitamin.

Drugs

Alcohol and smoking both have an adverse effect on our bones. In particular, the nicotine in cigarettes has an adverse effect on the cardiovascular system (the heart and the blood vessels), as well as on the respiratory system (the alveoli in the lungs) and on our breathing. Nicotine is clearly the recreational drug which our lifestyle will be better off without.

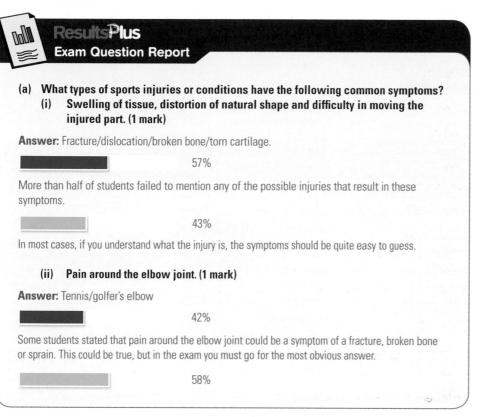

ResultsPlus
Exam Question Report

(a) **What types of sports injuries or conditions have the following common symptoms?**
(i) **Swelling of tissue, distortion of natural shape and difficulty in moving the injured part. (1 mark)**

Answer: Fracture/dislocation/broken bone/torn cartilage.

57%

More than half of students failed to mention any of the possible injuries that result in these symptoms.

43%

In most cases, if you understand what the injury is, the symptoms should be quite easy to guess.

(ii) **Pain around the elbow joint. (1 mark)**

Answer: Tennis/golfer's elbow

42%

Some students stated that pain around the elbow joint could be a symptom of a fracture, broken bone or sprain. This could be true, but in the exam you must go for the most obvious answer.

58%

ResultsPlus
Exam Question Report

(i) **What types of injuries are treated using RICE? (1 mark)**

Answer: soft tissue injuries

33%

Many students gave examples of specific injuries rather than the collective 'type' of injury requested. Make sure that you read the question and give what is asked for.

34%

(ii) **What do the letters RICE stand for? (1 mark)**

Answer: Rest, Ice, Compression, Elevation

31%

Most students answered this question correctly. As this question only asked what the letters stand for, it should have been easier to recall the knowledge required.

69%

Test yourself

1 One function of the skeleton is to enable movement.
   a State another function of the skeleton.
   b Give an example of the use of this function when participating in physical activity.

2 Joints are found in many places in the body but only in places where _____ meet.

3 Anita is 75 and she both swims and line-dances to keep herself fit and healthy. Of these two activities, _____ is the best for her bone health because _____ _____ activities are best for preventing the condition called _____.

4 She can also help to prevent the onset of this condition by making sure that in her _____ she has sufficient _____, which is a _____ found in such products as _____, _____ and _____.

5 Trampolinists may receive joint injuries as a result of taking part in their sport.
   a Name a joint injury.
   b State a sign or symptom of this injury.
   c How should a joint injury be treated?

Answers

1.1.1 Healthy, active lifestyles and how they could benefit you

1   D

2a

Physical	Social	Mental (or psychological)
• contribute to good physical health • improve performance • increase fitness • physical challenge	• make new friends • mix with others • meet old/current friends • develop teamwork/cooperation • work with others	• contribute to enjoyment of life • help the individual feel good • increase self-esteem and confidence • mental challenge • relieve and/or prevent stress and tension • aesthetic appreciation

b   Student's own examples.

1.1.2 Influences on your healthy, active lifestyle

1   B

2   Official, leader, volunteer

3   Elite/excellence. This is where individuals reach sporting excellence: it is at the peak of the pyramid because fewer people take part at this level.

4   B

5   2 hours

1.1.3 Exercise and fitness as part of your healthy, active lifestyle

1   B

2   C

3   B

4   How well a task is completed.

5   Improved fitness enhances performance.

6   Answer dependent on choice of activity.

7   Student's own examples.

8   agility, agility, balance, coordination, power, power, reaction time, speed

9a

	How speed is used in their performance
Athlete – sprinter	To get to the finish line first/faster/to get a good time/to win the race
Games player	To beat opponents to the ball / to lose / get free from opponents/to get around / dodge opponents (or equivalent)
Athlete – discus	To throw the discus further / increase power/to move faster across the circle/fast arm/reach the front of the circle at speed

b

	(i) Example of body parts being coordinated	(ii) Explanation of why example of coordination is important to performance
Athlete – sprinter	Arms and legs	Good technique to increase speed/power/drive
Games player	Feet and eye	Looking vision – at the ball and where to kick it
Athlete – discus	Arms and legs	Good technique to increase speed/power

NB: Example of body parts being coordinated must link to why coordination is important for FULL marks.

1.1.4a Physical activity as part of your healthy, active lifestyle

1   B

2   Skill – power (at the moment of impact);
     Test – sergeant jump

3

Test	HRE or SRF	What aspect of SRF or HRE does it test?	How do you carry out the test?
Illinois agility run	SRF	agility	Person lies face down on the floor at the start line. When signalled the person jumps up and runs around a course which involves many changes of direction. Person completes course as quickly as possible. Run is timed.
Hand grip test	HRE	muscular strength	Person squeezes a hand-grip dynamometer as tightly as possible. Take three measurements and record the best score.
Sergeant jump	SRF	Power	The person chalks their finger-tips and touches the wall as high as possible, stretching their arm above their head. Individual then bends knees and jumps, touching the wall at the highest point of the jump. Measure how high above the standing reach mark they jumped. Record the best of three attempts.

4a Barrie rests on Sunday.

b This allows his body to recover.

5 List any three of the following factors:
he gets what he wants from the programme (health/fitness);
he trains when he wants to;
he trains where he wants to (from home);
facilities – his bicycle;
cost – it's cheap;
he prefers to train alone.

6 Specificity

7 **Frequency** – Barrie applies this principle by training six days a week, which is more than enough.
Intensity – Barrie trains at about the same intensity each day, which is not enough to improve further.
Time – Barrie spends enough time (over 20 minutes) to keep fit.

Type – Barrie uses continuous training.

8 Progressive overload

9 **SMART** Specific, Measurable, Achievable, Realistic, Time-bound. Examples based on student's choice of activity.

1.1.4b Physical activity as part of your healthy, active lifestyle

1 cycling or brisk walking, anaerobic, interval, work, intensity, rest, fartlek, speedplay, hill, intensity, circuit, endurance, cheap, different, individual needs, principle, principle, specificity, balance

1.1.4c Physical activity as part of your healthy, active lifestyle

1 Prevent injury; help to perform better/give best performance or similar; prepare psychologically.

2 Pulse raising activity (jogging); stretching (exercises); specific skill-related practice; student's own example activities e.g. sprinter practise sprint starts.

3 D

4a anaerobically   **b** aerobically

c In the first 26 miles the intensity is not so high and they can cope with it. In the last 385 yards they sprint as fast as they can and so work anaerobically just as a sprinter would in a 100 metres race.

5 **A** = Carl   **B** = Zoe

6a Interval training

b Athlete A is performing periods of hard work followed by periods of rest (so his heart rate goes up when he is working hard and comes down when he is resting) which is the definition of interval training (what interval training is), so he is using interval training.

c Speed

d Skill-related fitness

e Specificity

7a Continuous training

b Athlete B is working at a much more constant pace; this is what continuous training is.

c Cardiovascular fitness or endurance

d Health-related exercise

e Aerobic

f The athlete is working at a steady pace so will not be getting out of breath or working above the 80 per cent threshold, and will normally remain between 60 and 80 per cent.

8 The thresholds of training

9 It is calculated by the formula 220 – your age x 60 per cent and 80 per cent, which gives the thresholds of training and the target zone.

10 The target zone

11 Either 12 or 13 minutes would be given a mark.

12 Either 12 or 13 minutes would be given a mark.

13 T for time

14a F for frequency

b Rest and recovery

15 I for intensity

16 Carl – 50 beats per minute

17 Carl's working heart rate goes higher over 150 or it goes out of the target zone. Zoe's working heart rate is quite steady/constant, while Carl's goes up and down.

18 Progressive overload

19 Carl will be working on muscular strength and Zoe muscular endurance.

20 Cross training

21 Individual needs

22 Main activity and cool-down

23 Pulse raising; stretching; specific skill-related practice

24 Any two from: prevent injury; prepare psychologically; improve performance

1.1.5 Your personal health and wellbeing

1 Starch and sugar

2 Simple

3 Protein

4 Fat

5 Helps bone strength

6 Prevent dehydration

7 Blood shunting

1.2.1 Physical activity and your healthy mind and body

1 Somatotype

2

Sport / activity	Somatotype
tennis/Wimbledon	mesomorphic ectomorph
100m sprint/Olympic final	mesomorph
football/midfield player	mesomorph
basketball/rebounder	mesomorphic ectomorph
bodybuilding/World's Strongest Man	endomorphic mesomorph
sumo wrestling	endomorph

3 Sprinter – mesomorph
Sumo wrestler – endomorph
Marathon runner – ectomorph

4a Obese

b Taking in the same number of calories while not using as many will result in those that are not used being stored as fat.

5 D

6 Damages the heart; damages the ability of the blood to carry oxygen; damages the blood vessels; increases blood pressure.

7 Damages the alveoli in the lungs.

8 Cirrhosis

9a To win; compete at the highest level; to make money; to be famous.

b Insomnia; irregular heart beat; increased heart rate; high blood pressure.

10 Narcotic

11a Trying to make sure that opposing players/teams are evenly matched.

b By skill/ability levels; weight; age or gender.

c Answer dependent on choice of activity.

d Warm up; wear correct clothing e.g. footwear for running; checking equipment e.g. batting gloves and pads for cricket; not wearing jewellery.

1.2.2 A healthy, active lifestyle and your cardiovascular system

1a The number of times the heart beats per minute.

b The heart will beat faster and stronger

c It will increase.

d Muscles need more oxygen and more carbon dioxide is produced and must be eliminated.

2 Lower resting heart rate and bigger stroke volume.

3 Rest allows the heart to increase in size and the number of capillaries to increase.

4 HDL

1.2.3 A healthy, active lifestyle and your respiratory system

1a The amount of oxygen consumed in recovery above that which would normally be consumed in the same time at rest.

b Anaerobically

c Lactic acid

d Reduce workload/or similar; breathe more deeply / cool down.

1.2.4 A healthy, active lifestyle and your muscular system

1 Hypertrophy

2a Position A: isotonic; Position B: isometric

3a Contracts, relaxes

b Extention/extending, flexion

c Quadriceps, hamstring

1.2.5 A healthy, active lifestyle and your skeletal system

1a Protection

b As a diver enters the water their skull protects their brain.

2 Two or more bones

3 Line dancing, weight bearing, osteoporosis

4 Diet, calcium, mineral, milk, cheese and yoghurt

5a Tennis elbow or golfer's elbow

b Pain on the outside of the elbow; pain on the inside of the elbow.

c Rest and RICE treatment

Index

Published by Pearson Education Limited, a company incorporated in England and Wales, having its
registered office at Edinburgh Gate, Harlow, Essex, CM20 2JE. Registered company number: 872828

www.pearsonschoolsandfecolleges.co.uk

Edexcel is a registered trademark of Edexcel Limited

Text © Pearson Education Limited 2010

The rights of Tony Scott have been asserted by him in accordance with the Copyright, Designs and Patents
Act of 1988.

First published 2010

12 11 10
10 9 8 7 6 5 4 3 2 1

British Library Cataloguing in Publication Data
A catalogue record for this book is available from the British Library.

ISBN 978 1 846905 88 9

Project management by Jim Newall
Edited by Helen Gough
Typeset by 320 Design Ltd
Original illustrations © Pearson Education 2009, 2010
Illustrated by 320 Design Ltd and Oxford Designers & Illustrators
Cover photo © istockphoto
Printed in Malaysia (CTP-VVP)

Acknowledgements
The author and publisher would like to thank the following individuals and organisations for permission to
reproduce photographs:

Action Plus Sports Images: Mike Hewitt 47 (2); Neil Tingle 70; **iStockphoto:** 66; Trevor Nielson 63; Chris
Schmidt 9; **Jupiter Unlimited:** Thinkstock Images 26; **Press Association:** T   47 (3). N   S
47; **Reuters:** David Grey 11

Figures
Page 12, Figure 2.16 from www.teachernet.gov.uk/-img/partnership%20Model.gif, Crown copyright, 2009,
Department for Children, Schools and Families

All other images © Pearson Education

Every effort has been made to contact copyright holders of material reproduced in this book. Any omissions
will be rectified in subsequent printings if notice is given to the publishers.

Disclaimer
This material has been published on behalf of Edexcel and offers high-quality support for the delivery of
Edexcel qualifications.

This does not mean that the material is essential to achieve any Edexcel qualification, nor does it mean that
it is the only suitable material available to support any Edexcel qualification. Edexcel material will not be
used verbatim in setting any Edexcel examination or assessment. Any resource lists produced by Edexcel
shall include this and other appropriate resources.

Copies of official specifications for all Edexcel qualifications may be found on the Edexcel website:
www.edexcel.com